Public Relations and the History of Ideas

This stimulating and innovative book explores ten great works, by well-known thinkers and orators, whose impact has been intellectual, practical and global. Most of the works significantly precede public relations as a phrase or profession, but all are in no doubt about the force of planned public communication, and the power that lies with those managing the process.

The works are stimulating and diverse and were written to address some of society's biggest challenges. Although not traditionally the focus of public relations research, they have all had a global impact as communicators and as the foundation for fundamental ideas, from spirituality to war and economics to social justice. Each addresses the implications of structured communication between organizations and societies, and scrutinizes or advocates activities that are now central to PR and its morality. They could not ignore PR, and PR cannot ignore them.

This book will be essential reading for researchers and scholars in public relations and communication and will also be of inter-disciplinary interest to study in sociology, literature, philosophy and history.

Simon Moore is Associate Professor and Chair in Information Design and Corporate Communication at Bentley University, USA.

Routledge New Directions in Public Relations and Communication Research
Edited by Kevin Moloney

Routledge New Directions in Public Relations and Communication Research is a new forum for the publication of books of original research in PR and related types of communication. Its remit is to publish critical and challenging responses to continuities and fractures in contemporary PR thinking and practice, and its essential yet contested role in market-orientated, capitalist, liberal democracies around the world. The series reflects the multiple and inter-disciplinary forms PR takes in a post-Grunigian world; the expanding roles which it performs, and the increasing number of countries in which it is practised.

The series will examine current trends and explore new thinking on the key questions which impact upon PR and communications, including:

- Is the evolution of persuasive communications in Central and Eastern Europe, China, Latin America, Japan, the Middle East and South East Asia developing new forms or following Western models?
- What has been the impact of postmodern sociologies, cultural studies and methodologies which are often critical of the traditional, conservative role of PR in capitalist political economies, and in patriarchy, gender and ethnic roles?
- What is the impact of digital social media on politics, individual privacy and PR practice? Is new technology changing the nature of content communicated, or simply reaching bigger audiences faster? Is digital PR a cause or a consequence of political and cultural change?

Books in this series will be of interest to academics and researchers involved in these expanding fields of study, as well as students undertaking advanced studies in this area.

Public Relations and Nation Building
Influencing Israel
Margalit Toledano and David McKie

Gender and Public Relations
Critical perspectives on voice, image and identity
Edited by Christine Daymon and Kristin Demetrious

Pathways to Public Relations
Histories of practice and profession
Edited by Burton Saint John III,
Margot Opdycke Lamme and Jacquie L'Etang

Positioning Theory and Strategic Communications
A new approach to public relations research and practice
Melanie James

Public Relations and the History of Ideas
Simon Moore

Public Relations and the History of Ideas

Simon Moore

Routledge
Taylor & Francis Group

LONDON AND NEW YORK

First published 2014
by Routledge

2 Park Square, Milton Park, Abingdon, Oxfordshire OX14 4RN
52 Vanderbilt Avenue, New York, NY 10017

Routledge is an imprint of the Taylor & Francis Group, an informa business

First issued in paperback 2019

Copyright © 2014 Simon Moore

The right of Simon Moore to be identified as author of this work has been
asserted by him in accordance with sections 77 and 78 of the Copyright,
Designs and Patents Act 1988.

All rights reserved. No part of this book may be reprinted or reproduced or
utilised in any form or by any electronic, mechanical, or other means, now
known or hereafter invented, including photocopying and recording, or in
any information storage or retrieval system, without permission in writing
from the publishers.

Notice:
Product or corporate names may be trademarks or registered trademarks,
and are used only for identification and explanation without intent to
infringe.

British Library Cataloguing in Publication Data
A catalogue record for this book is available from the British Library

Library of Congress Cataloging in Publication Data
Moore, Simon, 1961-
   Public relations and the history of ideas / Simon Moore.
      pages cm
Includes bibliographical references and index.
1. Public relations–History. 2. Rhetoric. I. Title.
   HM1221.M66 2014
   659.2–dc23
                    2013047287

ISBN: 978-0-415-63454-0 (hbk)
ISBN: 978-0-367-86741-6 (pbk)

Typeset in Times New Roman
by Taylor & Francis Books

For Isobel: keen reader and sharp questioner

Contents

Acknowledgments

I read the works in their original English or English translation: the latter an obvious limitation. Much of the value in this book lies with friends, colleagues and family who have directly or indirectly contributed to it. One of these is certainly Kevin Moloney of Bournemouth University and editor of the series in which this book appears. He must be credited with the idea of a book like this—though the choice of authors and responsibility for any accompanying errors are wholly mine. The idea was suggested in a lunchtime discussion after I presented a paper on Machiavelli's *The Prince* and Sir Thomas More's *Utopia*, at Bournemouth University's excellent annual conference on PR history. No series could desire a more thoughtful and insightful editor. My only regret is that we did not meet more often. This can also be said of the Routledge team: Jacqueline Curthoys, Sinead Waldron, Paola Celli and Kris Wischenkamper.

I am grateful to the anonymous reviewers of the original proposal, and also to Eric Austin, Bernie Kavanagh, Bruce MacNaughton, Ruth Macsween, Sean McDonald, Graeme Mew, Norine den Otter, Cliff Putney, Roger Richer, Javed Siddiqi, Terry Skelton, many other friends and my daughters Sophie, Imogen and Isobel. My wife, Dr. Sandra den Otter was invaluable to this project. Rarely do our scholarly paths cross but they did on this occasion, so I must offer academic as well as personal thanks.

1   PR and the history of ideas

Public relations (PR) has a history, and a pre-history. PR also must reflect social conditions. These commonplace remarks apply to many activities, but perhaps to PR more than many. PR must be highly alert to changes in the ways people see themselves collectively or individually, use technology and organize into groups to fulfil social functions. This very public activity leaves a historical trail that is intellectual, as well as tactical and technological.

PR's basic method has been followed from the earliest times, but most of that time it has not had the mixed blessing of a name. In the last century and a half its practitioners have had several names (including press agents, propagandists, publicists) that have changed with the emerging profession. The current name is highly unlikely to last forever, but the activity itself will continue to exist, generating new specialisms and tactics as organizations, societies and communication tools change. Change keeps the activity alert and alive. What is generally called PR, and its specialisms from crisis communication and public affairs to digital or entertainment PR, will thrive as long as an organization has something it needs to tell or hear from numbers of people, and must be alert to the best way of doing it.

To ignore the history and pre-history of an activity because it has or has not yet been named is of course absurd, as is accepted in most fields of study. The works in this book do not ignore the activity under consideration here, indeed cannot. They aimed to powerfully influence society and individual self-perception, which compelled the authors to consider how this could be achieved by the organizations best positioned to communicate their ideas. Through those ideas we can therefore see how public communication has been viewed and managed over millennia. Whatever the merits of this particular book, then, the works themselves deserve attention as PR artefacts, if for no other reason than their immense historical impact.

"Works" is used here in preference to "books" because it is more accurate, if unsatisfying. Some of these thinkers did not produce books, but essays, manifestos, theses, unfinished manuscripts, or observations that were recorded by others. Not all of it would count as scholarly output by today's unimaginative standards. A related question arises: why then these ten thinkers and not some other ten? Are they the *top* ten? The answer can only be that there is no top ten, but if there were, they would be vying for a place in it. Humans, thank goodness, cannot be ranked with such precision. Perhaps great thinkers can be ranked least of all as they have a habit of escaping the parameters that define greatness or influence at any particular moment. I have chosen people who are hopefully interesting, and have had an immense influence on organizations, society, power and eventually PR. There are others: not many, but others, and we must hope for further studies. While writing this book, I admit that I struggled and sometimes failed to ignore several other writers, one or two of whom I have previously written on: they include Kierkegaard, Machiavelli, Sir Thomas More, Wittgenstein. The ten works selected here demanded sufficient space and attention, and repaid it, but it was Kierkegaard, however, who in 1847 perhaps gave the clearest *raison d'être* for managed public communication, and thus for all books on the subject of PR: "There is a view of life which holds that where the crowd is, the truth is also, that it is a need in truth itself, that it must have the crowd on its side" (Kierkegaard, 2009, "There is a").

It is also fruitless to seek a single, unalterable, crystal clear point of origin or line of descent, as fruitless in PR as for any activity, technology or person. There are too many points of origin in all things, and to pick up one piece of bone or two or three in the vast Rift Valley of human history cannot lead us to an exact lineage—but we do come upon a broad downstream flow. For that reason, the ideas in these works pursued a set of themes that culminated in much of what we see today in the world of managing perception. Arguably, they were even more influential on PR than many modern scholars or commentators on the subject.

Perhaps a tentative, questioning, even impressionistic approach is best fitted for this book, as it should be for the field in general. PR knows, or should know, how difficult people are to pin down, to pin to products, ideas or desires. As a one-time historian who has written on past communication practice, I feel this and take comfort from it, for it is a sign of human autonomy, and one of the themes in this book is the impact of managed communication on human autonomy. Different views about this subject shaped the approaches of each work, perhaps also their philosophy as much as their views on its communication. Their approaches are often prescriptive, sometimes highly prescriptive, because they are not studying the world and its affairs, but offering concrete policies. There are no ivory towers here (although when I think of Michel de Montaigne's essays written in seclusion near Bordeaux, it must be said that at least some towers may have inspired works of value). Whether prescriptive or not, even these works could not avoid the possibility that individual autonomy, or contrariness, might assert itself; a contrariness which raises more questions than it answers and may ultimately confound attempts to manage public perception too closely or "scientifically". The noted twentieth-century historian G. M. Trevelyan made a useful observation about that tendency in a lecture to Britain's National Book League, two weeks after the end of the Second World War:

If you find out about one atom you have found out about all atoms, and what is true of the habits of one robin is roughly true of the habits of all robins. But the life history of one man, or even of many individual men, will not tell you the life history of other men. Moreover, you cannot make a full scientific analysis of the life history of any one man. Men are too complicated, too spiritual, too various, for scientific analysis.

(Trevelyan, 1945, p. 12)

Several of the works included here were written to impose more uniformity on societies, because the authors believed it would make those societies better places, especially those in times of turmoil—although when has there not been turmoil? Others were written to recover individual autonomy, for the same reason, and in the same conditions of turmoil or danger. The sheer variety of approaches they adopted suggests caution about their recommendations is sometimes necessary. We can be more definitive about their impact, and their influence on what may be called managed public communication, in the absence of PR's emergence as a name and profession though not as an activity, for that had happened already.

"Managed public communication" will at any event be the name risked most frequently here, for the reasons just given. On this question of naming, however, it must be admitted that I feel a little of what Edmund Blunden felt in his Great War poem, "Trench Nomenclature":

Ah, such names and apparitions! name on name! what's in a name?
From the fabled vase the genie in his cloud of horror came.

(Blunden, 1976, p. 90)

An alternative, "proto-PR", has strong claims but in this context seems too focused on the activities themselves. With the authors studied here we shall also explore their ideas for society and their relevance to PR. I hope the reader will see the implications of, say, Confucius' ideas for shaping social perceptions by managed public communication, and also see they are a direct ancestor of today's PR, and have something to say to it; but modern PR it is not. Naming is a necessary business, but not restrictive over-exactitude. A nomenclature-based system of taxonomy along Linnaean lines may obstruct historical understanding and ignore that debatable, blurry ground where ideas flourish and change emerges.

Nevertheless, all of these thinkers were deeply concerned with managing communication. None could escape it. Edward Bernays' "invisible government" (Bernays, 2005, "The conscious and") is frequently or always present, often very visible indeed in their work, even if it is missed in much subsequent scholarly analysis. In every case the thinkers see that managing social perceptions by large-scale communication is critical. It might be said that their own thinking would not have been complete without it, as much as it could be said that their thinking has shaped it in turn. As far as PR is concerned I argue these ten works have influenced our views of society, about what constitutes audiences, about what those audiences need to perceive and how they should learn of it, and which organizations must do that communicating. They form the intellectual, historical, origins of PR, but as I have already suggested, there are others.

"Master Zeng!" Confucius tells one disciple "All that I teach can be strung together on a single thread" (Slingerland, 2003, 4.15). This is true of the works studied here. Their big ideas are simple to grasp. Great ideas are often simple ideas, and can be simply expressed. Knots and complexities tied into them are occasionally the result of less liberated thinkers over-thinking that simplicity, or perhaps not daring to express it. Their underlying simplicity is one reason for their enduring popularity. It is also apparent to the student of PR that the existence and type of managed communication the authors envisaged for their "big ideas" tells us much about what kind of society was likely to be produced. The methods used to propagate the legitimacy of a society are almost as revealing as the big ideas themselves. Perhaps this understanding is underrated by any students of political economy, and any misguided practitioners of politics and business who persist in seeing PR as no more than a delivery vehicle, or something to do with marketing, even at the dawn of our Information Revolution, when its pervasive authority stares them in the face.

What useful PR-related themes appear in these works? They include some that trouble and some that empower the field today: the relationship between the individual and collective, expressed in the creation of audiences best fitted to receive certain messages; the balance of power between what may be called "scientific" and "non-scientific" approaches to public communication; views about the messages and media that best connect with target audiences; the problem of preserving liberty out of uniformity, and using communication to bring order out of chaos. All the works are interested in the communication relationship between State and citizen, or subject. This is because for many centuries only the State—and organized religion endorsed by the State—could marshal the resources for communication on a large scale, and also because the first need for society was order. This need preoccupies the earliest works studied here. How to achieve it? By propagating justice, or virtue, or piety, or harmony? We almost immediately face the issue of managing perception. Much later, a new factor appears: the rise of large-scale industrial production leading to intensive urbanization and more power to collectively manage perception. Most of the later authors—Mill, Hayek and Jung—view it as a problem; others—Marx, Engels and Gandhi—as an opportunity; von Clausewitz as a necessity.

I have chosen to look at each work separately and chronologically, rather than contrast and compare around particular themes. One reason for that is that the works are famous in their own right, and the product of highly original thought. I declare myself a confirmed believer that "Great" men and women exist in history, and are not just the product of particular social conditions. Two of the thinkers in this book are remembered and studied 2,500 years after they lived, and the others have developed or look like developing similar powers of endurance. It is valuable for PR as a scholarly and professional discipline to reflect on its own place in the work of these thinkers. Individual character matters: in their own lifetimes or posthumously several of the authors became PR assets, with valuable "PR equity" created from their real or imagined personalities by later generations. Another reason for this approach is that their ideas are often uniquely rather than collectively influential. Sometimes common themes develop, and are followed here, but others that must not be neglected are unique to the authors. This is why it matters to set the works in the context of their own times, so that we can understand which ideas transcend time and which ones (no less valuable) have something to offer because they are rooted in the author's contemporary experience.

Each work, being set in its particular time, represents a new stage for thinking about our relationship with managed communication. But Great persons do stand above trends to some extent. They create and build new edifices, as well as restore existing ones. Greatness is not always about newness. These are not necessarily flawless people and nor are their works, either by the less than perfect standards of our own bloodthirsty era, or more importantly by absolute and eternal standards of human decency, but that is to miss the point about their value as subjects for communication study.

So these authors and works, to repeat, tell us something about the origins of PR actions, ideas, about aspects of PR, because they offer prescriptions for society and cannot possibly avoid the question of communicating. Only one of the thinkers, al-Farabi, seeks to erase as much of it as possible, but naturally fails to do so altogether. The others recognize that overall control is more helpful, or propose ways of understanding and influencing the existing process. Their proposals for communication help or hinder their ideas, and we must remember that these were in almost every case adopted by or imposed on billions of people over time and space. What they prescribe for communication is in fact essential for their own success, and for the future of the people subjected to their recommendations.

For that reason, it seems helpful to include an approach that looks concretely at what is being said about key audiences and messages, strategy, media platforms, especially because another trait shared by these works is that they cannot avoid these subjects, although not necessarily in the order above because, to reiterate, the authors need to talk about communication between organizations and audiences. The organization that every author save Luther, Gandhi, and possibly Marx and Engels, makes their priority is the State, and what it must do to people in order to govern, sometimes justly and virtuously. The approach to "target audiences" grows a little more sophisticated over time, as we will see, gradually shifting in the search for a proper relationship between audiences and organizations.

We must not allow ourselves to think the works closest to us in time or space (wherever our particular space may be) are always the most relevant.

That is certainly not the case, especially as many principles and contradictions PR faces today were discerned early on in the rise of highly structured societies. I shall here insert a sentence by Churchill which I have used before: "That is the wisdom of the past, for all wisdom is not new wisdom" (Hansard, 1938, col. 367).

The works build a loose "philosophy of PR" from diverse subjects. Some describe an ideal society; others accept the world as it is, and offer guidance for reforming or prospering in it. Some take a collective, communal perspective; others concentrate on the individual. Several are actively political and address the public sphere; others advocate enlightenment from within. Two explore the intersection of society, communication and economics, and one the intersection of the State, communication and armed force. Several are directed at a particular culture or belief; others address humanity in the round. PR cannot altogether ignore such subjects.

Because the elements of PR are evolving in the works selected for study, it might in turn be asked if they have had a strong if overlooked influence on the history of ideas. I wish to suggest that they have. Much of the thinking and continuing impact of the people studied here is in fact determined—inevitably, as I have mentioned—by the activity we now know as PR, but which for much of human history had no settled name. These works are reacting to the control of communication by certain organizations; how those organizations were currently communicating, how they should communicate and the implications for the intended audiences. I wish to explore the ways their ideas are affected by their views on communication practice and its relationship to the problems of freedom. Those thinkers who actually advocate change are also proposing a communication strategy, often involving the creative use of multiple media platforms and the careful coordination of powerful messages. Many of those recommendations have left creative and often unexpected operational legacies for PR to consider, but it was clearly a two-way process. Public relations has indeed contributed to the history of ideas, which must be understood by scholars and students, in order to perceive the substantive nature of the field.

It is therefore possible that PR may help us reappraise the thinkers themselves. Plato for instance is considered an essentialist, seeking an underlying ideal and essence in all things. This made him attractive to later scholars in the Christian tradition and, as we shall see with al-Farabi, in Islamic philosophy. Plato's communication recommendations for a perfect State give a different impression of him, as indeed Plato himself does in *Parmenides*, when Parmenides famously points out to Socrates the problem of applying essentialism to: "Things that might seem absurd, like hair and mud and dirt, or anything else totally undignified and worthless". Plato's Socrates sticks to his principle, but adds: "Not that the thought that the same thing might hold in all cases hasn't troubled me from time to time" (Cooper, 1997, 130c–d). I suspect "Platonic PR" (I am being slightly facetious) also further exposes Plato's own struggles with this subject, by revealing a rather large difference between his philosophic pursuit of ideal forms and his practical pursuit of political objectives.

To return briefly to the issue of names, it will be seen that some of the reflections and proposals in the works would today be called propaganda, concerned with creating a publicity monopoly allegedly in the best interests of the audiences designed to receive it. There can be little doubt that PR's origins lie in this facet of its activity, traceable to the rise of sophisticated states with cities, bureaucracies and powerful religious organization. It is a progenitor of modern PR at least as much as nineteenth-century press agents, a fact that modern research into PR history now recognizes, inheriting a pioneering historical survey of the field by Edward Bernays in his 1952 book *Public Relations*. His 1928 book *Propaganda*, was partly a vain attempt to resuscitate a word that was coming into disrepute, and being attached by critics to one-sided attempts by governments, plutocrats and social movements to mislead or control society. The name public relations gradually rose in its stead. Bernays later took credit for this, although some people of his generation, including some in this book, continued using the word propaganda, often but by no means always in criticism.

Lesser themes may also be suggestive. One is that the works take what might be called an organic view of society, following the well-recorded classical tendency down to the time of Luther, to view society as a human body, enjoying good health and subjected to bouts of sickness. "O my poor kingdom, sick with civil blows!" cries Shakespeare's Henry IV, also succumbing to disease (*Henry IV*, Part 2, Act IV, Scene V) and in varying degrees this is the view taken by the first five works. Managed public communication was the spoon carrying philosophic medicine to the suffering State and its inhabitants. It was also the honey that would make the medicine palatable. We see this time and again in the attention paid in the earliest of these works to the language of the human body, of sickness and health, and their relationship with communication. Later the language changes, and the "common people" (to borrow from Confucius) or the people of lead or bronze (ditto Plato's *Republic*) begin to control more of their political, economic and religious affairs, and increase their own public communication activity, either as individuals or as members of a group. The works in this book move away from an organic perspective on communication, toward one that incorporates "nonnatural" constructions: bureaucracies, the social and other sciences and planning. The thinkers from Mill onward confront nascent or developed PR as an activity that impinges again and again on their thoughts in direct and obvious ways. They must face the question of what to do about it as a ubiquitous practice of highly technocratic societies.

A preoccupation that emerges in virtually all the works might, with care in some cases, be described as spiritual. When Confucius, al-Farabi or Gandhi or Jung, or even Marx and Engels write about communication, they are using it on behalf of the State to rebalance the spiritual wellbeing of their audiences, and through them society in general. Marx and Engels speak almost lyrically—if vaguely—about the personal happiness to be achieved. Confucius and al-Farabi are more precise, though their detail differs. Gandhi and Jung relate public communication much more directly to individual spirituality, bypassing the State and often critical of it. Luther would supplant media and messages current in his own time, and organized through the Catholic Church. In its place would be another possibility for public communication: more critical and intense, summoned from deeply personal experiences and spiritual quests. Hayek would roughly do the same, although his target is Statism and its adherents, and his objective is to restore another form of economic activity, partly in the belief that this would best preserve and grow individual freedom. Clausewitz is concerned with mobilizing the collective will of the nation, to sustain its forces in the tempest of what had become warfare between peoples, not merely dynasts and dictators. This idea is the progenitor of modern war as a comprehensive crusade to which a whole society is committed. It is the main lesson of *On War*, rather than weapons technology or the mathematics of maneuver. Perhaps the least spiritual in PR terms, other than Hayek, are Plato and Mill. In Plato's *The Republic*, religion and the myths of a people are not always treated as unassailable truths, but adapted to the media that communicates them and the political needs of the City. Mill's *On Liberty* concentrates almost wholly on secular, civic matters, and the problem of the mass media in civil society. He is not interested in tampering with Belief to perfect a State or "spiritualize" its citizens. It is worth understanding the spiritual dimension in these works, and how it is historically important to the PR function, whose most potent capacity is perhaps that it can rouse audiences by going beyond worldly matters of policies, products or service quality and price. It is mistaken to omit that dimension from studies of the field's potential, and the problems it raises, and the works here do not make that mistake.

A further refrain, which I hesitate to call "lesser", can be traced chronologically, and that is our changing view of communication itself, from being the servant of the Big Idea to becoming The Idea itself, which defines whether or not people are autonomous, and therefore free. Starting with Confucius, and ending with Jung, it is possible to follow this process, and the growing debate between what might crudely be called "virtuous PR" or "non-virtuous PR". By the twentieth century, the secular possibilities Plato identified could be comprehensively applied, and not only by States. That ushers in an additional refrain of the works: a slow awakening over the centuries to the consequences of intensified communication between organizations and audiences, between audiences and individuals. Of our twentieth-century great thinkers, Gandhi was most prepared to use it and accept the proliferation of the PR function as a tool rather than a threat. Hayek regarded it as a threat but one that must be harnessed by those who were threatened. Jung viewed it as a collectively imposed disaster for the individual psyche. In the nineteenth century the balance is somewhat reversed, with Clausewitz seeing managed public communication as absolutely necessary for the State, and therefore for the people in it. Marx and Engels turned it against the State and those who controlled it, while only Mill displayed real concern about its deeper consequences.

I will raise one more shared trait here, which unfolds as the works consider the problems and opportunities their ideas present to managed public communication. This is the complex interplay between virtue, truth, harmony, justice, hierarchy, the past, the future, individuality and belief in something—usually a religion and/or a particular social order. It might be said that all these topics exercise the authors, and the proportionate importance placed on each helped to decide the views of communication that was put forward by a society's leaders, until—as already noted—the last authors began to understand that communication itself was deciding those proportions as much as, or more than, the leaders themselves. A civic, political perspective is taken on these matters in every case, not a commercial one, with minor exceptions: Marx—in *Capital*—showed that he understood the "magical" element in the relation between consumer and commodity, but did not believe that it would have substantive reality or value in a perfected society. Hayek at least saw that civic and commercial "propaganda" or "publicity" was interrelated. Jung tended to ignore commercial publicity, although his work on symbols was influential in nongovernmental PR. These mainly political emphases on complex communication would now be considered insufficient: today most non-government PR practitioners would concur with Wittgenstein that: "The totality of true thoughts is a picture of the world" (Wittgenstein, 2001, p. 12), and take care to provide the totality, the truth, and a picture or two.

In human affairs, it is hard to develop much certainty without history. History casts light on the perennial elements of a particular subject, and those elements if consistent can harden into absolute certainties about the subject itself. In viewing communication over long spans of time, we should try to be ever more open to this approach, rather than one grounded in mathematical models or theory without historical analysis. The Prussian (later German) General Staff were in no doubt about it. Their first great reforming Chief of Staff, General Karl von Muffling, established four departments: the first three concerned aspects of army organization, the fourth and smallest dealt with history, from which doctrine could be developed (Lee, 2005, p. 15). Eventually, in the 1914–18 First World War, the German General Staff further extended its control over society by establishing an extensive propaganda program, and taking control of large sectors of the economy. It might be fair to say that PR itself is following a similar path: government policies, business products and public reputations regularly submit to its priorities. Any serious study of the world's public affairs cannot now be pursued without sophisticated knowledge of PR, knowledge that was being developed by the thinkers studied here.

Did these thinkers "invent" PR? No. Were they aware of the importance of what is *now known* as PR? Yes, without any doubt. They were aware that strategically managed communication by organizations, and all that that involves, cannot avoid shaping society and individuality. They therefore had ideas for managing it properly. Public relations must study the history of their ideas to recover this part of its inheritance.

References

Bernays, E. L. (1980) *Public Relations.* Norman: University of Oklahoma Press.

——(2005) *Propaganda.* With an introduction by M. C. Miller. Brooklyn, NY: Ig Pub.

Blunden, E. (1976) "Trench Nomenclature." In B. Gardner (ed.) *Up the Line to Death: The War Poets, 1914–1918.* London: Methuen.

Cooper, J. M. (ed.) (1997) "Parmenides." In *Complete Works.* Indianapolis, IN: Hackett Publishing Company, 359–97.

Hansard. (1938) 5th Series, Munich Agreement. October 5. *339*, cols. 360–70.

Kierkegaard, S. (2009) *The Crowd is Untruth.* Translated by C. Bellinger. New York: Vanessa Myers.

Lee, J. (2005) *The Warlords: Hindenburg and Ludendorff.* London: Weidenfeld & Nicolson.

Slingerland, E. (trans.) (2003) *Confucius Analects.* Indianapolis, IN: Hackett Publishing Company.

Trevelyan, G. M. (1945) *History and the Reader.* Cambridge: Cambridge University Press.

Wittgenstein, L. (2001) *Tractatus Logico-Philosophicus.* Translated by D. F. Pears and B. F. McGuinness. London: Routledge.

2 Virtuous PR

Confucius (c. 551–479 BC), *Analects* (c. first quarter of fifth century, BC)

Confucius and PR

The PR value of Confucius is not lost on China today, although he was discredited in the Cultural Revolution of the 1960s. Now, the admired sixth-century sage, scholar, gentleman and official is an important part of China's public diplomacy. He has been the name on it since 2004, since when over three hundred Confucius Institutes and the same number of Confucius Classrooms have opened worldwide. Their job is to educate global communities about China and offer cross-cultural exchanges, in common with other institutional ambassadors like the British Council or Germany's Goethe Institut. An observer describes Confucius today as "part of a broader soft power projection in which China is attempting to win hearts and minds for political purposes" (Paradise, 2009, p. 649). In especially important regions like Africa, Confucius institutes are proliferating on university campuses across the continent, often in the wake of state visits and trade agreements (Han Shih, 2013, p. 4). He is embraced by business as well. In 2013 a luxury hotel themed for him opened in his birthplace of Qufu in eastern China. "Expect to see", promised the advance publicity "contemporary Chinese design touches, such as red lacquer panels, combined with the three key principles of Confucian philosophy: order, harmony and hierarchy" (Life & Leisure, 2013, p. 2).

What Confucius might think of this perhaps depends on how we think of him. Certainly, it is hard to think of him—and perhaps any great philosopher—lifting (or lowering) himself from contemplating "order, harmony and hierarchy" and taking an interest in the business of managed public communication. For thousands of years rulers have revered him almost as a Saint, who was followed by disciples and not students. For thousands of years, China's rulers sacrificed to Confucius as the Sage of Culture, and the transmitter of ancient virtues. He *became* spiritualized public relations, part of the Chinese ritual calendar, embodied in icons with "godlike visual features" (Murray, 2009, p. 373). For 2,500 years he has been one of the ways China's rulers are legitimated.

If saintliness were the whole of it, there would be no more to be said. "Under such a definition a Saint is no match for us. He is an ideal which we can only behold" (Hattori, 1936, p. 97). The Japanese sinologist (and interwar nationalist) Hattori reminds us that so venerable a Confucius would in the end give us little chance to develop, to learn for ourselves, and Confucius constantly said he was learning, and that what he had learned others could equally learn, and apply to the practicalities of government. For that reason we might prefer to think of him as Sage or Statesman, as principled pragmatist or cloistered philosopher, but also as one who felt he was Divinely directed. Hattori writes of this latter conviction "The personality of Confucius is very gracious, but it has a foundation of extraordinary power, and although cool and quiet it contains extraordinary zeal and enthusiasm" (Hattori, 1936, p. 108).

His life certainly contained these disparate elements, and what united them and took them into the practical realm were his ideas about government and managing public communication. In that, Confucius might be said to have gone a step further than those who now see the institutes that bear his name as political in purpose, without crediting the deeper communication strategy that is the foundation, expression and identity of public diplomacy. After all, phrases like "soft power" or "public diplomacy" are themselves PR products; acceptable, high-purposed names for reputation-based PR practiced by governments to communities abroad.

On the face of it the *Analects,* the collected sayings of Confucius and also some of his students, is not a very promising source for studying managed public communication. It is a guide to personal virtue, inward looking, emphasising individual qualities like virtue and modesty. Confucius seems almost "anti-PR" when he praises the "ultimate Virtue" of an ancient leader who "declined rulership of the world three times", and "remained unpraised because the common people never learned of his actions" (Slingerland, 2003, 8.1).

Yet Confucius was also concerned with good government. "When our Master arrives in a state", one of his students asks another, "he invariably finds out about its government. Does he actively seek out this information? Surely it is not simply offered to him!" The answer is that he obtains it by "being courteous, refined, respectful, restrained and deferential" and then the revealing conclusion: "The Master's way of seeking it is entirely different from other people's way of seeking it, is it not?" (Slingerland, 2003, 1.10). In this passage we learn of the importance of government to the *Analects,* and receive an early glimpse of the part played by communication, which is developed into something more far-reaching as the book proceeds. Confucius was political. Revered as a Sage and an exponent of rites, but seeking ministerial responsibilities. He had practical knowledge of the realities of power at that time—in one case apparently foiling a plot to kidnap his Master, the Duke of Lu, and shaming the would-be kidnapper (Dubs, 1946, p. 276). Almost alone of the thinkers discussed here his chosen career was a state administrator "with the practical grasp of a genius" it has been claimed (Dubs, 1946, p. 280), and "not a mystic figure" (Dubs, 1946, p. 282).

Confucius himself said that practice decided personal character (Slingerland, 2003, 17.2). The practice of good government inevitably drew the management of collective opinion into his observations and dicta, alongside the communication of personal example and humility. He believed his prescriptions would be unhelpful unless taken up by governments and reflected in their public communication. For that reason his long exile from political power tested his patience (Slingerland, 2003, 9.9). There had been no omens that a Sage King like those of old was returning to employ Confucius, the practical administrator.

Confucius believed that: "Working from the wrong starting point will lead to nothing but harm" (Slingerland, 2003, 2.16). His starting point was the education and upbringing of rulers, gentlemen and other people of talent appointed to serve them. Remaking a society by communicating to its youngest members is often the preserve of a revolutionary person or a revolutionary idea—and observable in today's PR campaigns aimed at schools by energy corporations, ideologically motivated governments and environmental non-profit organizations. It occurs in several other works studied here, but Confucius was neither radical nor revolutionary.

Analects was set down in the fifth century BC, arranged into its final form in the later third century BC. Confucius' first followers may have written it out at the start of this timespan, known as the "Warring States" period. Confucius himself lived in the preceding "spring and autumn" period, also a time of turbulence between rival rulers, and as with other works studied here, the author (or follower, or amanuensis) seeks to understand, restore or rebuild the individual and the State. The purpose of the *Analects* is classically conservative, to renew the future by diligently learning from the past. "I am not someone who was born with knowledge", he said, "I simply love antiquity, and diligently look there for knowledge" (Slingerland, 2003, 7.20). Confucius believed "natural, spontaneous, unselfconscious harmony had once prevailed during the reigns of the ancient sage-kings Yao and Shun, as well as during the Golden Age of the 'Three Dynasties'—the Xia, the Shang, and the Zhou" (Slingerland, 2003, Introduction). Restoring harmony and balance to individuals, using lessons learned from history, would restore Virtue to rulers and their people. This is the theme of the book, which is in part a guide to the ways it could be accomplished.

Confucius and his key publics: rulers, gentlemen and common people

How has Confucius defined the audiences that matter to him? Segmenting and targeting audiences is not a refined art in *Analects*, nevertheless it could not be altogether avoided as Confucius sought to change State and Society. We do not hear much of markets or merchants, Marx's "bourgeoisie". Confucius has little to say in favour of pursuing profit; a little more on its power to disrupt the pursuit of virtue (Slingerland, 2003, 9.1). In Book 9, Chapter 1 it is recorded he gave his views on profit, the Heavenly Mandate, and Goodness, but no detail is added. Elsewhere, it seems profit seeking is becoming the province of "petty persons"—not traders but officials, and even learned persons—who are incapable of resisting the temptations of salary or profit

(Slingerland, 2003, 15.32). The short shrift extended socially to "merchants, mechanics and others" lasted long after Confucius. In the eighteenth century they occupied the third and last rank of society, according to two British observers who published in 1804, and those of civil and military rank "affect to despise equally" "those whose lives are occupied in the concerns of commerce" (Alexander & Mason, 1988, Plate LXII, p. 130).

So much for the private sector and its dangerous impact on good government; we hear more positively about "gentlemen" and rulers who should be cultivated, modest, virtuous and pious. A gentleman "understands rightness, whereas the petty person understands profit" (Slingerland, 2003, 4.16). The gentleman's role is to set an example to the largest audience, who are unpromisingly described in Slingerland's translation as the "common people". The rulers asking Confucius for advice view common people—overwhelmingly peasant villagers—as little more than a resource, or a source of unrest. One ruler sets out what he wants from them when he asked Confucius what he must do to induce their obedience (Slingerland, 2003, 2.19); another lord wishes them to be "respectful, dutiful and industrious" (Slingerland, 2003, 2.20).

Confucius himself stressed "ritual propriety and deference" (Slingerland, 2003, 4.13) from rulers as well as subjects. A young person—and presumably gentleman in this context—"should display a general care for the masses but feel a particular affection for those who are Good" (Slingerland, 2003, 1.6), and in the words of one of his students, he "takes pity on those who are incapable" (Slingerland, 2003, 19.3). Needless to say, it would disrupt propriety to include common people as a whole in government, except for talented individuals who could be found among them. Confucius accepts the ancient heavenly mandate of rulership but takes pains to point out that common people must not be neglected, telling one student that a State needs sufficient food and armaments, but most important of all the people's confidence (Slingerland, 2003, 12.7).

The best approach to the people was to show self-sacrifice (Slingerland, 2003, 13.1); setting an example of self-control (Slingerland, 2003, 12.18); piety and benevolence, and "to bring succour to the multitudes" (Slingerland, 2003, 6.30). Even this much consideration raised questions. One of Confucius' students asked if such a ruler could be called good, suggesting uncertainty about the subject (Slingerland, 2003, 6.30). Confucius' ideas about common people must have been striking for the time. When either his own or the State's stables burned, it was noted that he asked if anyone was hurt, and not about the horses (Slingerland, 2003, 10.17). "If the common people's needs are satisfied", one of Confucius' students suggests to Duke Ai, "how could their lord be lacking?" (Slingerland, 2003, 12.9)

The objectives: *dao*, *li* and *ren*

Dao—the way of virtue—must be present in government. The common people, meanwhile, "can be made to follow it, but they cannot be made to understand it" (Slingerland, 2003, 8.9). They could follow it, not by force and punishment, but by witnessing State virtue through its management of language, ritual and music, and Confucius' views on this are examined later. He drew his precepts from his studies of ancient ruling virtues, when the two sage-kings "Shun and Yu possessed the entire world and yet had no need to actively manage it" (Slingerland, 2003, 8.18). Book 10 of *Analects* gives some details of the practical example and consideration educated officials should display, saying for instance that when villagers "were performing the end of year exorcism" Confucius "would stand on the Eastern steps of his house dressed in full court regalia" (Slingerland, 2003, 10.14). He did not eat or drink to excess; was careful to make sacrifices on the proper occasions, to wear the correct formal clothes for the correct ceremonies; to leave drinking ceremonies—which could get out of control—after the elderly people had left; to bow twice to departing messengers. Slingerland explains that a double bow expressed "respect to the acquaintance to whom he was sending the complimentary regards" (Slingerland, 2003, 10.15). "When the Way prevails in the world", Confucius concluded, "commoners do not debate matters of government" (Slingerland, 2003, 16.2). Popular sentiment is not a reliable guide to rule, though this presumably also applies to the glib gentleman or profit-seeking ruler. "When the multitude hates a person, you must examine them and judge for yourself. The same holds true for someone whom the multitude love" (Slingerland, 2003, 15.28).

Confucius, more in common with his near-contemporary Plato, and for that matter Shakespeare and many others, parallels the body of the citizen or subject with the organism of the State. A virtuous and harmonious mind and body produce a virtuous and harmonious State. Political upheaval is constrained by filial respect imbued at an early age. Like Plato, the Confucian State cultivates youth carefully. A properly raised youth who respects elders "is disinclined to defy his superiors stirring up rebellion" (Slingerland, 2003, 1.2).

The goal of *dao*, or The Way, is to find the way to learn, to live, to understand, to achieve virtue, to be good, to study the arts, govern and to die (Slingerland, 2003, 7.6). All well and good, a realist like Machiavelli might respond, but what about the business of staying in power? Power is a matter of practical policy; of projecting puissance, ceremony and personality to your subjects, allies and rivals; of security, stability, survival. Government is about the steps that must be taken with the institutions and people who are important to it, not inward cultivation of harmony and virtue. A State would certainly be risking much if it pinned its future on *dao*; so might have said that exiled participant in the brutal politics of the Renaissance and student of the no less brutal realities of ancient Roman rule. One or two others studied here might have nodded with Machiavelli, either turning like him to statecraft or policy; or objecting that tinkering with the spirituality of a State's subjects served no purpose, and neither did advocating inner change by unrealistically embracing antique principles—whether a divine authority, or particular civic ceremony. We do not return in these pages to something resembling Confucius' highly inward-looking approach until we reach Carl Jung. Nevertheless, in large part *Analects* concerned itself with restoring harmony in the State, and *dao* was the recommended method, and so readers cannot evade the question of how the State should convincingly communicate The Way.

Nevertheless, the opening lines of Book 1 of the *Analects* are not complimentary in their references to communication, particularly when "The Master said, A clever tongue and fine appearance are rarely signs of Goodness" (Slingerland, 2003, 1.3); and here Slingerland notes "This suspicion of glib speech and superficial appearance is found throughout the *Analects*" (Slingerland, 2003, 1.3), as when "The Master said, 'Clever words confound virtue'" (Slingerland, 2003, 15.27). Communication was often a subject that made Confucius impatient. "Of what use is 'eloquence'? If you go about responding to everyone with a clever tongue you will often incur resentment" (Slingerland, 2003, 5.5).

Caution and suspicion about communication's ability to deceive is another recurring theme in virtually all the works studied here and especially in relation to government, and it is edifying to see it raised in the fifth century BC. As Confucius develops his thinking, however, we learn that the management of public communication has a more positive part to play. It does so through *li*, which is the path to *dao*, and whose "root meaning is close to 'holy ritual', 'sacred ceremony'" (Fingarette, 1966, p. 58) but which is taken to mean "rites", "rituals of propriety" (Li, 2007, p. 311). *Li* is as important to the State as it is to the young people referred to earlier.

The Master said, "To guide a state of one thousand chariots, be respectful in your handling of affairs and display trustworthiness" (Slingerland, 2003, 1.5). "Showing" respect and "displaying" trustworthiness in the affairs of State are closely connected to *li*, as practiced in past times with "harmonious ease" and regulated by the rites, according to one of his students, Master You. "It is precisely such harmony that makes the Way of the Former Kings so beautiful" (Slingerland, 2003, 1.12).

If *dao* is The Way to personal virtue and ultimately a virtuous State; and *li* a means of achieving it, the third important concept in Analects is *ren*, interpreted as "humanity, human excellence" (Li, 2007, p. 311). *Li* and *ren* seem to be interdependent: the way to one is through the other, individually and communally (Li, 2007; Yu, 1998).

Confucius applies these principles to government in greater depth in Book 2 of the *Analects*, in which we begin to see the task of public communication in achieving *dao*, *li* and *ren*. It appears that achieving these things is sufficient unto itself: "One who rules through the power of Virtue is analogous to the Pole Star: it simply remains in its place and receives the homage of the myriad lesser stars" (Slingerland, 2003, 2.1). An example must be set, though, and—as we shall also see with Plato—Confucius does not believe excessive law-making can accomplish the task: the attempt to legislate people to Virtue was evidently as well-developed then as it is today. Regulations coerce and do not teach the common people, Virtue expressed in ritual inculcates shame and self-improvement (Slingerland, 2003, 2.3).

Confucius advocated personal piety expressed in the observation of rituals and good teaching, beginning in the family, and extending into government. He constantly warns against insincerity (see for example Slingerland, 2003, 1.8, 15.6) and advocates seriousness and propriety (see for example Slingerland, 2003, 1.13; 2.4). His approach requires an intricate self-control in many aspects of life, extending to a gentleman's home fittings (Slingerland, 2003, 1.14). In this he has a total vision of communication, embracing the private and the public. The policies that promoted propriety had to be communicated by advancing upright people in government (Slingerland, 2003, 2.19), which again is not a policy Machiavelli would find realistic, perhaps with justification. Confucius' support for sincere ritual and filial piety does at least provide a consistent standard by which upright officials can be identified. In that sense it resembles Plato's idea of selecting rulers through a lifetime's observation, and leads to Confucius' version of a teacher-scholar-philosopher king, deserving of reverence (Slingerland, 2003, 2.20).

Ritual must not mean rigidity. Sincerity comes before rigidity, a principle which Confucius advocated (and also Christ—"the Sabbath was made for man, not man for the Sabbath"). In festive ceremonies "it is better to be spare than extravagant. When it comes to mourning, it is better to be excessively sorrowful than fastidious" (Slingerland, 2003, 3.4).

In Confucius' lifetime rulers could not resist tampering with ritual, could not leave their own feelings private, and wrote themselves into the process, therefore cheapening it. While making offerings to their ancestors, for instance, the three aristocratic families who rivalled the Duke of Lu included an ode referring to them, which was probably performed by a chorus as the sacrificial vessels were being cleared (Slingerland, 2003, 3.2).

Confucius naturally disapproved. The ritual was being adjusted to interpose the families over the legitimate ruler—showing that while Confucius taught *dao*, *li* and *ren*, he was aware that ceremonies could be misused for a distinct and sometimes dangerous political purpose. He warns, in a general observation probably also directed at the three families he criticized: "A man who is not Good—what has he to do with ritual? A man who is not Good—what has he to do with music?" (Slingerland, 2003, 3.3).

The relationship between ritual and music, and their power to shape perception, were for Confucius matters of state politics as well as private life, and many of his ideas connect music, ritual and government. He liked music and understood the influence it could have over him, "a wondrous ocean of sound!" (Slingerland, 2003, 8.15).

Knowing its influence helps to explain Confucius' concern to restore ritual and music to their virtuous sphere because, Slingerland notes, "It is clear that by the time of Confucius the Zhou ritual tradition had been severely corrupted, and that this corrupted tradition was in turn responsible for leading the vast majority of people astray" (Slingerland, 2003, Introduction, "It is clear that").

In the eleventh century BC the Duke of Zhou had reflected on the fall of rival states and as Regent introduced rituals with the intent of expressing virtue in concrete form to the people. This theme, the establishing of virtue by ritual, appears in the early histories of other rulers, as an essential for building stable societies, inculcating a shared and settled sense of purpose, belief, virtue and identity. One such was Numa Pompilius, venerated by the Romans as their second king after Romulus. Public music, poetic language, and ritual interested Plato as well. In his *Republic,* Socrates suggests basing them on a "noble lie", conjured from religious myth to serve the State's purposes. Confucius wants to make the same assets work for the State, but only by restoring real virtue to them.

Communicating therefore sets itself the objective of *dao,* by the correct use of *li* and *ren,* and this concern with appearances, conduct and ceremony is the heart of Confucius' interest in government. "I hate it", he said, "that purple has usurped the face of vermillion, that the tunes of Zheng have been confused with classical music, and that the clever of tongue have undermined both state and family" (Slingerland, 2003, 17.18). Such powerful media could not be overlooked in any practical plan for constructing a contented society. To him, they were extremely powerful forces in state affairs: vehicles for the communication of virtue, but also of corruption.

The media

Language, and ritual language

Perhaps the most important example of Confucius' concern with public communication was to be what one of his students called "trustworthy in speech" (Slingerland, 2003, 1.6). A gentleman is "simply scrupulous in behaviour and careful in speech, drawing near to those who possess the Way in order to be set straight by them" (Slingerland, 2003, 1.14), he is "slow to speak, but quick to act" (Slingerland, 2003, 4.24).

Confucius reverenced the past as a guide, believing former ages, showed more restraint, measuring their words to fit their deeds (Slingerland, 2003, 4.22). He was deeply concerned with the measured use of words, which he connected to learning, ritual, to music and thence to political order and social harmony. His first act, if restored to office, would be to correct the use of names, as the incorrect use of ancestral descent and family relationships in the leading families of Lu was infiltrating public ritual, confusing public perception and leading to political instability. Confucius traced a connection between incorrect names, to incorrect speech, to lifeless rituals and music, inappropriate legal enforcement until "the common people" lose direction and purpose (Slingerland, 2003, 13.3).

Simplicity of language also reflected virtue in people and society through them. Elaborate, ornate sentences were not needed (Slingerland, 2003, 15.41). Confucius' view of public communication was to reach virtue through simplicity and sincerity in language, music and ritual.

Confucius took care to use classical pronunciation when conducting ritual (Slingerland, 2003, 7.18), managing perception by managing language as well as words.

Ritual acts

"If those above love ritual, then the common people will be easy to manage" (Slingerland, 2003, 14.42). Confucius frequently said that ancient ritual was an essential tool of State, and by his time had become an extremely intricate process for the conveyance of legitimacy.

Great weight was placed on rituals surrounding funerals, venerating ancestors and spirits, dictating clothing, diet, the numbers of baskets and jars used or when sacrifices should be blood, raw meat, partially or fully cooked; and the ways officials were approached (Slingerland, 2003, Introduction, "We might be tempted to label"). "A principal duty of the Chinese court was to provide ritual feasts for the gods and spirits at imperial altars and temples" (Wilson, 2002, p. 251). Such responsibilities are common to most states, pre-modern or modern. In China it was developed to a complex extent. Ritual also conveyed the virtue of the ruler. It was in that sense a form of transparency, and it must be conducted in a certain way, assuring observers that your respect for ritual mirrored your inner character: "it was necessary that the king perform it with sincerity", Slingerland points out (Slingerland, 2003, Introduction). "How could I bear to look upon such a person?" asked Confucius, referring to ungenerous, impious, insincere rulers (Slingerland, 2003, 3.26).

Confucius' attention to ritual extended, it was noted earlier, to making an example of his own clothing. He dressed appropriately for feast days and recommended conducting affairs of state in the correct attire (Slingerland, 2003, 15.11).

Public ritual must therefore be bigger than individual taste and ambition, and if conducted properly bestowed harmony, wisdom and perspective. Without ritual, a respectful person becomes exasperating, a careful person timid, a courageous person unruly and an upright person inflexible (Slingerland, 2003, 8.2).

Rites operated at the level of the State, the community and the family. Filial piety was the first step in respecting the rites on the path to *dao.* Children were to serve, bury and sacrifice to their parents "in accordance with the rites" (Slingerland, 2003, 2.6). In the community the festivals and ceremonies must be upheld and country gentlemen must demonstrate respect for the ritual and legitimize it to the common people. In government, the ritual and language of ceremonies must not be contaminated by extravagance or political propaganda, and observed with dignity.

It is plain that emphasis on ritual is not confused with an obsession with over-elaboration and points of detail. Confucius sought to simplify and clarify approaches to ritual; to restore its virtue and value. Ritual was not to be used to make personal propaganda, but conducted with modesty and reverence to awaken virtues and traditions much bigger than the ruler's caprices. The Way absolutely precluded writing one's own personality into the ritual. Confucius noted that in ritual "extravagance leads to presumption" and frugality to shabbiness, with the telling addition that shabbiness was better than showing presumption (Slingerland, 2003, 7.36).

Music and time

Musical references and analogies are frequent in the *Analects*. Slingerland writes that Confucius viewed music, and poetry, as a model for "self-cultivation: starting in confusion, passing through many phases and culminating in a state of wu-wei [an effortless manner of doing things] perfection" (Slingerland, 2003, 3.23). Liu Baonan (1791–1855), the noted student of Confucius, surmised that Confucius' famous advice to: "Find inspiration in the *Odes* [poetry], take your place through ritual, and achieve perfection with music" (Slingerland, 2003, 8.8) meant "to have one's moral qualities refined by music and brought to completion" (Cai, 1999, p. 325).

Unsurprisingly, Confucius' preferred musical media were the compositions for the sage-kings of old. The Shao court music was to him "perfectly beautiful and also perfectly good"; whereas the music of a more belligerent king was "perfectly beautiful, but not perfectly good" (Slingerland, 2003, 3.25). Music, then, could be morally good and bad.

Slingerland describes the State management of music in China as an "important moral task" (Slingerland, 2003, 9.15). This line perhaps understates its political importance. Music was far too potent to be left to its own devices and records show States took a close political interest in it, evidently monitoring changes and sometimes intervening to manage the medium, as Confucius himself did: "Only after I returned to Lu from Wei was music rectified, with both the Ya and Song put into proper order" (Slingerland, 2003, 9.15). Confucius' views on music are not unknown today. Like Plato's treatment of poetry, music and ritual in *The Republic*, the *Analects* concerns itself with the communication of useful values, with the difference that Plato is ready to adjust old pieties to meet the musical needs of his perfect city-state, while Confucius seeks authentic, original music to embed the historical roots of piety in his own State. Nevertheless, Confucius has views on the political and moral impact of music that Plato would recognize: "Prohibit the tunes of Zheng, and keep glib people at a distance—for the tunes of Zheng are licentious, and glib people are dangerous" (Slingerland, 2003, 15.11).

One further significant feature of Confucius' statecraft and communication is his view of time. The communication he preferred was after all time-honored and time-conquering. Rituals, language and music are most virtuous when longevity is a part of their legitimacy. The idea that transient issues could be of any value has little attraction: the peace and harmony of the body and the government depended on patience and veneration of ancestors, family and ancient example. Confucius wanted to draw the flush and fever out of communication, to slow the pulse of the State by ritual, music and managing its language to reflect older values and not current rivalries. In this approach, body, soul and State are connected. When was a man truly filial? If he does not alter his father's ways for three years after his death (Slingerland, 2003, 1.11). How long would it take to create a good State? Confucius endorses a saying: "If excellent people managed the state for a hundred years, then certainly they could overcome cruelty and do away with executions" (Slingerland, 2003, 13.11). However, a "true king" could restore goodness in one generation (Slingerland, 2003, 13.12). The first fruits of good leadership would appear much sooner: "Having been instructed by an excellent person for seven years, the common people will be ready for anything, even the taking up of arms" (Slingerland, 2003, 13.29). Confucius' felt his own statecraft and philosophy meant he could do the job more quickly were he given the chance: "If someone would simply employ me, within a single year I could put things into some kind of order, and within three years the transformation would be complete" (Slingerland, 2003, 13.10). Slowing time down encouraged the sort of communication that inspired *dao, li* and *ren*.

When would the king, lord or gentleman equipped with *dao, li* and *ren* be ready to rule or administer the affairs of state? Again, Confucius' takes the long view. Plato details a testing program of education in *The Republic*, where those who have passed assume leadership at fifty years of age. As Cai points out: "Confucius does not prescribe a definite timetable" (Cai, 1999, 320), although an informal suggestion may be offered in Confucius' account of his own trajectory, in which—also at fifty years old "I understood Heaven's Mandate" (Slingerland, 2003, 2.4). At fifty, however, he had no official position.

Perhaps Confucius venerated a past that did not exist, or was less pure than he believed. Perhaps he was right to do so, because the perceived image of the ancients mattered more than any reality. Perhaps, in the end, it was that perception of the past that mattered most in his world, and using that perception to create a better society was a practical, and worthy, endeavor. The risk, which is repeated elsewhere in these pages, lay in attempting to embody virtue in personal example—leading, even in the case of Confucius himself, to a cult of personality—and by the potential paradox of state control of popular media to publicize virtue. In Confucius' case this control seems relatively light, much lighter than the management of communication in a China today that continues to venerate him. His lightness of touch will be less apparent in later thinkers.

References

Alexander, W. and Mason, G. H. (1988) *Views of 18th Century China: Costumes, History, Customs.* London: Studio Ed.

Cai, Z. Q. (1999) "In Quest of Harmony: Plato and Confucius on Poetry." *Philosophy East and West*, 317–45. Confucius Institute.

Dubs, H. H. (1946) "The Political Career of Confucius." *Journal of the American Oriental Society*, 66(4): 273–82.

Fingarette, H. (1966) "Human Community as Holy Rite: An Interpretation of Confucius' *Analects*". *Harvard Theological Review*, 59(1): 53–67.

Han Shih, T. (2013) "Hard Investment versus Soft Power." *South China Morning Post*, July 22, p. 4.

Hattori, U. (1936) "Confucius' Conviction of his Heavenly Mission." *Harvard Journal of Asiatic Studies*, 1(1): 96–108.

Li, C. (2007) "Li as Cultural Grammar: On the Relation between Li and Ren in Confucius' *Analects*." *Philosophy East and West*, 57(3): 311–29.

Life & Leisure (2013). "Confucius Say Stay Here." *Australian Financial Review*, July 19, p. 2.

Murray, J. K. (2009) "'Idols' in the Temple: Icons and the Cult of Confucius." *The Journal of Asian Studies*, 68(2): 371–411.

Paradise, J. F. (2009) "China and International Harmony: The Role of Confucius Institutes in Bolstering Beijing's Soft Power." *Asian Survey*, 49(4): 647–69.

Slingerland, E. (trans.) (2003) *Confucius Analects*. Indianapolis, IN: Hackett Publishing Company.

Wilson, T. A. (2002) "Sacrifice and the Imperial Cult of Confucius." *History of Religions*, 41(3): 251–87.

Yu, J. (1998) "Virtue: Confucius and Aristotle." *Philosophy East and West*, 48(2): 323–47.

3 Noble falsehoods and PR

Plato (c. 428–347 BC), *The Republic*
(first half of fourth century BC)

Communicating an ideal

A century after *Analects* was first set down (though not in its final form) *The Republic* opens with several acts of managed public communication, when Socrates visits Piraeus to offer a prayer to the goddess, see a parade and watch a festival. So it begins with a civic display, and civic society is the theme of the book.

Like parts of Confucius' *Analects*, *The Republic* of Plato is constructed from a series of questions and answers. Like *Analects*, the subject is the State, in this case the city-state. Rather like *Analects*, Plato's *Republic* will "contrive to spread happiness throughout the city by bringing the citizens into harmony with each other" (Plato, 1997, 519e). In *Analects* social harmony requires personal virtue, piety and respect for tradition. In *The Republic* it is achieved by grooming the best possible leaders and policies for the State they will lead. Each question to Confucius produces an answer; those to wise Socrates in *The Republic* produce counter questions that in the end generate a series of proposals. The first are rules from the mouth of the Sage, the second is a debate about government. *The Republic* believes virtue depends on government institutions. *Analects* believes that individual virtue will improve collective government. These alternatives often appear in the works studied here.

Both books were written in particularly unstable times, but Plato has turned Confucius the other way round, and does not much reference history either. Citizens exist to serve and support the greater needs of the government. Most are too variable to change or to be consistent and wise leaders: afflicted with old age, ignorance, drinking, although some perhaps are ennobled by reflection. Their inner life is scarcely a factor in the conduct of government. Only a few were fit to build a civic superstructure in which to shape society. In a culture that put great importance on public rhetoric, the management of public opinion by these few is an inevitable corollary. Socrates pays considerable attention to the Republic's citizens as receivers of key messages from their leaders; his idea will not work if the citizens do not see themselves in the way he sees them. The reader is invited to consider citizens as various categories: warrior-rulers and guardians, merchants, husbandmen, craftsmen; people of gold, silver, bronze and iron; people who prefer opinions over knowledge; young and old; men and women; profit-lovers and honor-lovers; all moving closer or further away from the god-given sunlight that reveals perfection to the human soul. Some groups are more likely than others to produce people equipped to achieve perfection and therefore govern. In each citizen, however, lies a danger to happiness and the happiness of the Republic: a civil war in the soul between the parts that are irrational and rational, and the spirited part "boiling and angry" that fortunately "aligns itself far more with the rational part" (Plato, 1997, 440e). The Republic must help its citizens establish "friendly and harmonious relations" between all three parts (Plato, 1997, 442c). It does not seek equality although it does seek happiness. Plato knows some people will always be much cleverer than others. Popper observes that "Plato, and his disciple Aristotle, advanced the theory of the biological and moral inequality of man" (Popper, 2011, "Reacting against this").

How does Plato represent public communication between these unequal groupings, and the conflicted soul? What account of this appears in *The Republic*, itself an act of supremely influential and long-lasting public communication? According to Plato, speaking through Socrates, the task of "bringing the citizens into harmony" must be achieved "through persuasion or compulsion" (Plato, 1997, 519e) and this idea guides his views of managing public communication. Karl Popper's great critique *The Spell of Plato*, the first volume of *The Open Society and its Enemies*, accepted the honest motive of securing happiness for citizens, but believed that "the medico-political treatment which he recommended, the arrest of change and the return to tribalism, was hopelessly wrong" (Popper, 2011, "In the light of"). True, Plato's Socrates and friends are constantly revisiting and tinkering with social categorizations, with the aim of "fixing" them unchangeably in the city's structure, though children showing talent have the chance to move further up the ladder. The result looks something like tribalism, if not totalitarianism.

On the other hand, the British theologian Benjamin Jowett, in his famous 1881 translation of *The Republic*, also reminds readers of "the likeness of God", which Plato "saw dimly in the distance", "the likeness of a nature which in all ages men have felt to be greater and better than themselves". However it has been regarded, that likeness "is and will always continue to be to mankind the Idea of Good" (Plato and Jowett, 1990, Introduction and Analysis). Do Plato's views on managed public communication throw light on these alternatives, and what are *The Republic*'s implications for communication itself?

Managing perception

A similar clash of possibilities seems to appear in his plans for public communication. Plato's *Republic* and Sir Thomas More's *Utopia* (1516) agree that communication in civic society can be used to deceive. In both books the management of an organized State presents a moral challenge to just ruler-ship and communication. Yet we can also see similarities between *The Republic* and Machiavelli's *The Prince* (1513), who advises rulers how to manage media to hold onto power by using deceit if necessary, rather than by cultivating virtue in individual citizens. *The Republic* therefore contains a tension between an abuse of power and a little necessary dishonesty. What role does communication play in resolving or aggravating this, and in creating a Republic closer to Popper's or Jowett's interpretation?

Through the famous dialogue featuring Socrates whom he followed in his youth, Plato justifies the Republic he has in mind partly by identifying a still unsolved problem in the relationship between communication and the city-state. This problem is pursued in some detail in Book III, but also appears elsewhere. Socrates begins this strand of the dialogue, which we shall follow as it runs or reappears in the book, by implying rather like Machiavelli, that just or unjust leaders are not the issue. The system itself is the issue, says he. Plato and Socrates look to introduce a *just* system rather as Confucius culti-vates virtue within everyone, including leaders: by controlling the commu-nication process. In *The Republic*, Socrates puts a just and unjust man beside each other at the head of the State, an unjust person who "will act as clever craftsmen do" (Plato, 1997, 361a), and a just man "who is simple and noble and who, as Aeschylus says, doesn't want to be believed to be good but to be so" (Plato, 1997, 361b). Socrates shows how it is possible for bad rulers to be pro-tected by virtuous public acts, and the deceiving role of communication is opened up. He recognizes the problem of an unjust man who wants not to *appear* unjust but to *be* unjust. What does such a man need to do in his public communication? He needs, Glaucon tells Socrates, to build a "reputation" for justice. And how does he accomplish that? By public acts that mislead the polis about his true nature and placate the gods themselves. An unjust ruler may exploit his public reputation, marry whom he likes, give his daughter to anyone he chooses, and also make contracts and partnerships with anyone he chooses. He will become a rich man because he has no hesitation in acting unjustly. Meanwhile, his virtuous public acts will be made known in the polis (the city-state to which most Greeks belonged). He makes "adequate sacri-fices to the gods, and sets up magnificent offerings to them" and will be better able to serve those gods, and also "the human beings he's fond of" (Plato, 1997, 362b–c). These public acts, rather than private virtues, make him more likely to be the gods' favorite. What of the just man who chooses not to be believed as good by his public conduct, a person like Socrates who is less ostentatious about publicizing his own virtues? If that is what he wants, says Socrates with customary provocativeness: "[W]e must strip away his reputa-tion, for a reputation for justice would bring him honor and rewards, so that it wouldn't be clear whether he is just for the sake of justice itself or for the sake of those honors and rewards" (Plato, 1997, 361b–c).

What is the result of this refusal to develop a public reputation? That of the two, the just man: "Though he does no injustice, he must have the greatest reputation for it" (Plato, 1997, 361b–c). Thus the trap public communication contains for good civil government is recognized, almost at its birth: the power to deceive about the character of the communicator.

The remedy for this seems more extensive in Plato's approach than in Confucius': centralized communication must be more involved in the promotion of just government. In Confucius, the State also has a part to play in communication as the guardian and manager of certain public rituals that complement private rituals in order to encourage virtue. His, though, is a less State-controlled system since the managed public communication in the *Analects* is tempered by historic and heavenly precedents, and community participation.

Plato's parallel with the pragmatic Machiavelli seemingly ends here for his remedy to the problem is not dissimilar to the one offered by Sir Thomas More, or Marx and Engels in the *Communist Manifesto.* It is no less than a perfect State that has little need to succumb to communication's many lures, and test the city's laws, because its guardians need to "believe throughout their lives that they must eagerly pursue what is advantageous to the city and be wholly unwilling to do the opposite" (Plato, 1997, 412d–e). Plato achieves this "by imagining a set of institutions designed to educate citizens to believe that the laws are sacred and permanent" (Cohen, 1993, p. 314).

The institutions are famously led by people chosen from an elite group who are carefully observed at all ages to ensure their fitness for the task. Communication is placed in a helpful relationship with this government, because it is confined presumably to what is needful rather than what is artful, and because "neither compulsion nor magic spells will get them to discard or forget their belief that they must do what is best for the city" (Plato, 1997, 412e). Communication has the capacity to deprive people of a true belief— Socrates calls it "theft" and places it alongside the dangers of magic and compulsion. Persuasion can make people change people's minds, as can the other thief—forgetting: both equipped to take "away their opinions without their realizing it" (Plato, 1997, 413b). Magic, too, involves casting a spell of pleasure or fear—managing perceptions by influencing emotions is not a task PR has rejected.

The communication environment is strewn with such snares for the citizen's soul. All the more important, then, to produce leaders impervious to these dangers: tested, filtered and true. What is true? In the life of the city, it is "to believe the things that are" (Plato, 1997, 413a). Leaders able to do that must be tested by, presumably, citizens, for their power to believe what is and disbelieve what is not; to withstand the magical and worldly temptations contained in communication. Tested by continuous observation, by physical challenges, by exposure to fears and pleasures, those who pass through the process successfully become, at the age of fifty (Plato, 1997, 540a) the rulers and the guardians of the State.

The reward of such an ideal is a city where managed communication appears hardly necessary, but *The Republic* still cannot let go of the subject, and for two reasons—to discourage incorrect sentiments, and encourage correct ones. What do Socrates/Plato have to say about this?

Today, one of the biggest risks of *The Republic's* ideal is the creation of a society in which certain kinds of civic communication are controlled or forbidden. If the ideal State fails to convince a citizen, the absence of free communication means totalitarian subjection for that particular person. Whatever its power to mislead, liberty of communication in public life seems essential to a free—or free-ish—society, more even than debates between individual liberty and community, or liberty and equality. *The Republic* itself accepts this risk to liberty of communication. Socrates raises it in Book II when he presents, then counters the assertion that the perfect gods, the best possible beings, perpetuate belief in them with an untruth—by their ability to shape-shift and appear as less perfect forms of existence. This illusion, this deception "through sorcery" (Plato, 1997, 382a) is nevertheless acceptable because it is not "true falsehood" not a falsehood of the soul—because, where "no one is willing to tell falsehoods to the most important part of himself about the most important things" (Plato, 1997, 382a).

The gods—and on this plane the perfected rulers and guardians of the city—are above committing such a true falsehood, but the god–endorsed practice of deceiving by illusion suggests other falsehoods are acceptable. There are for instance times when a lesser category, "falsehood in words", is useful for everyone (Plato, 1997, 382b): "Isn't it useful against one's enemies? And when any of our so-called friends are attempting, through madness or ignorance, to do something bad, isn't it a useful drug for preventing them?" (Plato, 1997, 382c).

Finally, Plato suggests: "By making a falsehood as much like the truth as we can, don't we also make it useful?" (Plato, 1997, 382c) This is not a sentiment the less scrupulous PR practitioner would object to, and *The Republic* builds upon the lesser falsehood idea later in Book III when Socrates famously discusses and finally proposes devising "one of those useful falsehoods we were talking about a while ago ... one noble falsehood that would, in the best case, persuade even the rulers, but if that's not possible, then the others in the city" (Plato, 1997, 414b–c).

The main elements of a noble falsehood (practical Socrates gives a Phoenician story as an example of one with this potential) could present the reality of life as a dream and the myth or falsehood as the reality. In this way it would explain why the city is worth defending, and through mystic evocation legitimize its social and physical structure. The "magic" and "theft" inherent in communication was to be neutralized or perhaps (in the case of creating a suitable founding myth to last for generations) at best controlled by the rulers or guardians and those auxiliaries who support their "convictions" (Plato, 1997, 414b).

The sample falsehood Socrates offers uses myths from another culture and people rather than—more dangerously—his own. It is interesting, tantalizing, and not quite an aside, to note the concern of his listeners. A reception that sometimes greets public relations claims today, if its arts are explained to non-practitioner audiences without resort to the creative media that breathes life into them. "It isn't for nothing that you were so shy about telling your false-hood", says one of Socrates listeners (Plato, 1997, 414e). "So," asks Socrates "do you have any device that will make our citizens believe this story?" (Plato, 1997, 415c) No, it is replied, "but perhaps there is one in the case of their sons and later generations and all the other people who come after them" (Plato, 1997, 415d).

Managing media

To begin with, Socrates does not discuss exactly how this myth was to be communicated, since he does not seem interested in specific communication media, and perhaps overlooks the influence it would have on his proposal, though it seems clear that the poets will be involved in promoting the noble falsehood, as they were involved in the civic and religious communication of many pre-modern societies. He says, "let's leave this matter wherever tradition takes it" (Plato, 1997, 415d) and moves on to describe the ways in which the Republic could repel outside enemies and "most easily control those within, if anyone is unwilling to obey the laws" (Plato, 1997, 415e), namely by building a camp for the rulers on a commanding site, a camp that would ensure they were "kindly allies" to the citizens rather than "savage masters" (Plato, 1997, 416b).

How were the dangers in public communication to be constrained? In this we see that Socrates was not after all really prepared to leave tradition to its own devices, and is drawn into the subject. We have suggested that Socrates was aware of the social power exerted by at least two media—music and poetry—as his listeners also seem to be, and states right up to the present certainly have been. He recognizes that the noble falsehood must be communicated—vaguely leaving the content to tradition, as noted—but also that the most popular media also represents a threat to the Republic, for it is hard to con-trol. As one of Socrates' listeners says (Adiemantus): "lawlessness easily creeps in there unnoticed", seeps into ways of life, private contracts, laws and government "until in the end it overthrows everything, public and private" (Plato, 1997, 424d). "Yes," Socrates agrees, "as if music and poetry were only play and did no harm at all" (Plato, 1997, 424d).

He invites us to conclude that "All poetic imitators, beginning with Homer, imitate images of virtue and all the other things they write about and have no grasp of the truth" (Plato, 1997, 600e). Truth is the great goal, the necessity for a Republic capable of rising above the flaws contained in democracies, aristocracies, oligarchies, tyrannies and monarchies. For that reason "it is in music and poetry that the guardians must build their bulwark" (Plato, 1997, 424c). Above all, the rulers must watch these unpredictable arts:

> Above all, they must guard as carefully as they can against any innova-tion in music and poetry or in physical training that is counter to the

established order. And guarded against corruption. And they should dread to hear anyone say:

People care most for the song
That is newest on the singer's lips

(Plato, 1997, 424b)

Creative novelty in attractive media is potentially disruptive to the Republic. Evidently this has been known—and feared—for a long time by people and governments and from Plato to Jazz, Rock and Roll, Punk or Rap. Socrates reemphasizes: "the guardians must beware of changing to a new form of music, since it threatens the whole system. As Damon says, and I am convinced, the musical modes are never changed without change in the most important of a city's laws" (Plato, 1997, 424d).

In Book X Socrates is more emphatic: "If you admit the pleasure-giving Muse, whether in lyric or epic poetry, pleasure and pain will be kings in your city instead of law or the thing that everyone has always believed to be the best, namely, reason" (Plato, 1997, 607a).

In addition to repelling dangers contained in powerful media, as the discussion proceeds, ideas emerge for communicating the values of the Republic to its citizens, which make use of the same media. Here too, Socrates is not in the end content to let tradition take its course. Poetry has the power to express the ideal Form, including the ideal city, and Battin points out that this power over the ideal explains why Plato places it in the hands of the city's rulers: "Only the philosopher, and then only after long and rigorous practice of dialectic, can hope for such a view; the common man, chained in the cave, is virtually ignorant of the Forms, and has no way of seeing them" (Battin, 1977, p. 169).

The rulers must promote the law and perfect nature of the city, and to do this they must use cultural media—I use the term to describe the artefacts and activities in society preferred by different audiences for exchanging information and absorbing values. This includes music and poetry under controlled conditions in which "hymns to the gods and eulogies to good people are the only poetry we can admit into our city" (Plato, 1997, 607a). It also includes children's games, for don't lawless games make "it impossible for them to grow up into good and law-abiding men?" (Plato, 1997, 424e) "But when children play the right games from the beginning and absorb lawfulness from music and poetry, it follows them in everything and fosters their growth, correcting everything in the city that may have gone wrong before" (Plato, 1997, 424e).

"[T]he start of someone's education", Socrates avers, "determines what follows. Doesn't like always encourage like?" (Plato, 1997, 425b) He later clarifies that music, poetry and physical training should be extended to women as well (Plato, 1997, 452a), and by extension the right to be guardians.

The management of message-carrying media appears again in Book V, which establishes the role of women in the Republic. Eugenics is also recommended, bringing together the best men and women "as frequently as possible" (Plato, 1997, 459d) and taking away the children of good parents to be raised by the State, and the rest to be hidden "in a secret and unknown place" (Plato, 1997, 458e). The fortunate children will learn their lessons by play rather than force, because "nothing taught by force stays in the soul" (Plato, 1997, 536e). To improve the chances of producing such children, general promiscuity is discouraged to ensure the success of the Republic, by making marriage "as sacred as possible. And the sacred marriages will be those that are most beneficial" (Plato, 1997, 460c). Shortly after this remark, Socrates provides more detail: "Therefore certain festivals and sacrifices will be established by law at which we'll bring the brides and grooms together, and we'll direct our poets to compose appropriate hymns for the marriages that take place" (Plato, 1997, 459e).

If nothing else this passage, which is perhaps slightly cynical to modern eyes, shows some at least in the pre-modern world understood how ritual ceremonies and other public events were valuable for managing secular behavior, and were pragmatic about exploiting them as a pseudo-religious platform of special effects on behalf of the State. The passion in an event encourages young people to follow the crowd, to "say that the same things are beautiful or ugly as the crowd does, follow the same way of life as they do, and be the same sort of person as they are" (Plato, 1997, 492c).

For this reason the energy in these occasions will also be exploited to reward heroes in battle: "we'll honor them at sacrifices and all such occasions with hymns, seats of honor, meats, and well-filled cups of wine", says Socrates (Plato, 1997, 468d), perhaps thinking of the ceremony and parade he had attended earlier that day. After all, what is the effect on young people at a "public gathering of the crowd" where "the very rocks and surroundings echo the din of their praise or blame and double it … What private training can hold out and not be swept away by that kind of praise or blame and be carried by the flood wherever it goes" (Plato, 1997, 492c). Here is an account of the threat and opportunity of spectacle, rather than the magic and theft inherent in wordplay. As we have seen, Socrates' ideas for channelling control and content of such public occasions through the rulers show he fully understood the opportunities as well as the threats.

What can communication students make of *The Republic* in the twenty-first century? Naturally our knowledge of recent history may lead us to think that a perfect State—not necessarily the one Plato envisages—justifies a degree of control over the messages and the media. This is certainly practiced in societies of different stripes, whether in the doctrine of political correctness, in corporate control of much of the main media, or in the surveillance carried out by State security organizations. The pursuit of "a more perfect union" by all states and super-states, it seems, still cannot be achieved without attempting this management in lesser or greater degrees. Perhaps this raises the question of whether it can be achieved at all. Jowett traces Plato's influence over centuries of utopian literature, to which we might also add Karl Marx and Engels in this book, but it is at least debatable whether attempts to realize these purest conceptions have contributed much to the sum of practical human happiness. Managed public communication can be achieved to an extreme degree, and the social structure reordered; to that extent Plato was espousing distinct possibilities. Yet it is hard to claim that these accomplishments have come close to fulfilling their ideals, or are pleasant to those at the receiving end. Perhaps Jowett is being just when he writes:

> To us the State seems to be built up out of the family, or sometimes to be the framework in which family and social life is contained. But to Plato in his present mood of mind the family is only a disturbing influence which, instead of filling up, tends to disarrange the higher unity of the State.
>
> (Plato and Jowett, Plato, *Introduction & Analysis*)

Although alarmed by such consequences, Popper grants that Plato's intentions are pure, as we have seen, agreeing: "his wish to make the state and its citizens happy is not merely propaganda" (Popper, 2011, "In the light of"). That said, much of Plato's ideal depends on a one-way, censored use of media (in this case ritual, other ceremonies, poetry, and music) to ensure his Republic is not contaminated by baser appeals to the passions. The city that pursues Plato's objective is one where the media must be controlled by its perfect rulers and edited for content to reinforce agreement in the city's own perfection. This does not immediately strike one as a place where a gadfly like Socrates would be particularly happy. He was after all too much even for the rulers of argumentative Athens. The nearest any polis came to it was Sparta, whose social structure was one basis for *The Republic*, but was not emulated by their neighbors, though it was sometimes admired, and sometimes feared.

While communication media attracts little positive enthusiasm, and more caution, the message of *The Republic* is certainly communicated in a very definite social structure, again one that influenced More in *Utopia*, although his ideal guardians were craftsmen and yeoman farmers. In Plato's *Republic* the particular temptations inherent in communication are countered by measures against the temptations of wealth and property. Virtually all property is common property. The temptation of gold is lifted from More's and Plato's rulers by changing its image from an attraction to a pollutant. In this way, Socrates suggests, rulers will have time to rule liberated from the plots and envy that comes with ownership and acquisition.

The Republic is a perfected State maintained by the careful management of media to make people respectful of its laws and believers in its noble falsehoods. It is impossible to imagine Confucius taking such a pragmatic approach to myths, legends and ceremonials. For him happiness lies in absorbing virtue from belief in the divine and historic rituals that hedge individual life. Plato channels virtue through the city. Disallowing some forms of the most popular media, tinkering with religion and managing their content is justified by the idea that the city cannot be wrong, for it is "completely good", which is to say "wise, courageous, moderate, and just" (Plato, 1997, 427e). Interfering with the law becomes unnecessary in these circumstances, and Socrates appears to conclude that laws and constitutions are less important than the wisdom of the superior rulers, or managing the media he has identified. In a badly governed city passing laws accomplishes nothing; in a good city it would not be needed as the citizens can work it out for themselves (Plato, 1997, 427a). Courage, for instance, exists in the city, because the city knows what civic values are to be feared (in other words respected and preserved) because "they are the things and kinds of things that the lawgiver declared to be such in the course of educating it" (Plato, 1997, 429c). The principles of the Republic are best absorbed this way, via public communication acting like a dye, fixing truths that are hard to wash out (Plato, 1997, 430a). The foundation of the city's justice and prosperity is managing media to communicate values and myths as an ideal and natural state of affairs, not by imposing or debating laws: "If Glaucon [Socrates' interlocutor] is to be convinced of the happiness of the just life, he needs to be shown that the Guardians' restraint can be *natural*" (Mara, 1983, p. 599).

In this ideal Republic then, the segmented sections of society are content; the warring parts of the soul have been reconciled by men and women who have been schooled and selected for the task over their whole lives to rule the city. Music, poetry and public ceremony are high among the means needed to draw the citizen out of the darkness of the cave, and its shadows and illusions, helping to lead them, and most of all their rightful rulers into the bright light where all can be understood for what it really is (Plato, 1997, 514–18), and the soul can achieve fulfillment. In his city, there is rational prosperity under sound governance, a place for everyone and everyone happy in the place they find for themselves, or are born into, and perhaps—perhaps—that would even include Socrates.

Nevertheless, the consequences for managed public communication, and therefore for society, must be unattractive to anyone schooled in ideas about relatively free expressions of opinion, relatively free markets and relatively free social mobility. It supports Popper's view that whatever the spiritual ideal Plato was pointing the way to earthly totalitarianism, justified to serve what is perceived as an absolute social good. Socrates does not seem defensive about such a proposal, as someone might be today, with greater theoretical or practical knowledge of intensive State propaganda and managed messages. *The Republic* raises the possibility that messages and media can be coordinated, not used ad hoc for flawed rulers or warring cities, but to consistently and repetitively promote a disciplined ideology for a non-existent utopian State. This vision has attracted many people, with occasionally disastrous consequences. It is not the only occasion managed public communication pursues perfection at the expense of other messages; but it must certainly be among the first.

References

Battin, M. P. (1977) "Plato on True and False Poetry." *The Journal of Aesthetics and Art Criticism*, 36(2): 163–74.

Cohen, D. (1993) "Law, Autonomy, and Political Community in Plato's Laws". *Classical Philology*, 88(4): 301–17.

Mara, G. M. (1983) "Politics and Action in Plato's Republic." *Political Research Quarterly*, 36(4): 596–618.

Plato. (1997) "The Republic." In J. M. Cooper and D. S. Hutchinson (eds) *Complete Works*. Indianapolis, IN: Hackett Publishing Company, 971–1223.

Plato and Jowett, B. (trans.) (1990) *The Republic*. Champaign, IL: Project Gutenberg. Retrieved from www.gutenberg.org/catalog/world/readfile?fk_files=3274525.

Popper, K. (2011). *The Spell of Plato*. Vol. 1 of *The Open Society and its Enemies*. London: Routledge.

4   The problem of perfection

Abu Nasr al-Farabi (c. 875–c. 950/1AD), *On the Perfect State* (c. 950)

PR in an ideal world

Is managed public communication needed in a perfected society? Plato's *Republic* says yes, but a case could be made that PR activities are always aiming for their own extinction, since achieving their particular objectives would make them unnecessary. The tenth-century logician and philosopher Abu Nasr al-Farabi (sometimes called Alpharabius in the West) raises this possibility by mapping the path to perfection in human society. His methods are less comfortable to twenty-first-century readers than are those of Confucius, who sought inward change, or Plato who was interested in a more secular state structure.

Al-Farabi used logic to describe a divinely sanctioned State. What then is left for earthly PR to do? Would it no longer need to exist? *On the Perfect State* answers this question, and the answer reverberates into the present, and later attempts to establish societies liberated from error.

This is perhaps the most abstract work considered here, and perhaps the most ambitious attempt to imagine a fully realized society. Al-Farabi was one of the few equipped to make the effort. The twelfth-century philosopher and astronomer Maimonides praised his works on logic as "fine flour" and the only ones worth reading (Hammond, 1947, p. xiii). He also contributed to music, alchemy, physics and psychology, travelling extensively across the Middle East, living in Baghdad, Damascus and in Aleppo at the Emir's court.

For all his brilliance, al-Farabi requires staying power from PR-inclined readers, and perhaps would even have tested Confucius and Plato, as his starting point was highly—and to us painfully—crablike. Like Confucius and Plato, he wrote at a time he felt was politically unstable. His aim was to bring vulnerable states as close to perfection as possible. This is extremely ambitious compared to Confucius' more attainable truth and virtue, or Plato's civic truth and justice—which were ambitious enough.

To dissect and divine a perfect state, al-Farabi starts at perfection's ultimate source. He then ranks all things above, in and after existence, from perfect to less perfect to imperfect, and finally comes to the State, or city, which "ought to be arranged in the same way: all its parts ought to imitate in their actions the aim of their first ruler according to their rank" (al-Farabi, 1985, 15.6; p. 239). Nor can the Ruler "just be any man" because he—and to al-Farabi it is certainly a He, and ideally one only—must be, by logic, the first in rank in the city as both a part and also a microcosm of the order of things in the Universe: "(a) he should be predisposed for it by his inborn nature, (b) he should have acquired the attitude and habit of will for rulership which will develop in a man whose inborn nature is predisposed for it" (al-Farabi, 1985, 15.7; p. 239). Moreover: "This is the sovereign over whom no other human being has any sovereignty whatsoever; he is the Imam; he is the first sovereign of the excellent city, he is sovereign of the excellent nation, and the sovereign of the universal state" (al-Farabi, 1985, 15.11; p. 247).

This absolute faith in divine predisposition is a departure from *The Republic,* which at least had an earthly vetting process, and even Confucius' Sage-Kings, who were more Sage than Saint. *On the Perfect State* is not congenial to secular democrats and/or supporters of unfettered communication. Contemporary approaches to ordering and ranking, while equally if not more intense, are at least secular and possibly scientific. Al-Farabi's faith-based taxonomy respected the prime precept of the Medieval world, whether Muslim or Christian, European or Asian. The growing Age of Faith had much to recommend it to the minds of philosophers, after all. In Europe the Church had stabilized the chaos of the Early Medieval, guided and regulated the volatile affairs of princes, produced most of the continent's greatest art and architecture and by the ninth century helped cities, trade and financial networks recover from a near-total collapse at the end of the Roman Empire. The Islamic world had also embarked upon a similar, and perhaps much greater efflorescence. Baghdad, where al-Farabi spent most of his adult life, and where most of the book was written, was on the way to becoming the largest city on earth and drew scholars from across the widening Islamic world.

Nevertheless, al-Farabi is more familiar to us than might be supposed. This is not to say he rejected faith. In the first chapter of *Perfect State* he describes the utterly perfect "First Existent", building on Plato's idea in *Laws* of "the first cause of the birth and destruction of all things" (Plato, 1997, 891e). Yet perfection brings religious questions. A thing cannot be utterly perfect by faith alone, but because logically, in terms of pure reasoning power, the First Existent could scarcely be anything else, regardless of faith. What then is the role of faith? Is it to set limits on what can be communicated between the State and its subjects? Al-Farabi seems to say that it is.

The idea that perfection is apart from us, not part of us, is a troubling deduction whose echoes are famously found in, among others, the later logician Wittgenstein's *Tractatus Logico-Philosophicus* (completed in 1918 and published in 1921). This work was made for a different purpose but took a similar approach. It is helpful to compare the two in order to better understand *Perfect State,* and the part played by managed public communication. Wittgenstein and al-Farabi try to cut out as much static as they can and reason towards what knowledge we are able to know.

The opening of both books demonstrates the power of both authors, and a telling dissimilarity. Wittgenstein begins "1st The world is all that is the case" and then "1.1 The world is the totality of facts, not of things" (Wittgenstein, 2001, p. 5). Wittgenstein begins with where we are now and tries to discover what is known, and what is not. After that point, Wittgenstein famously concludes, "7. What we cannot speak about we must pass over in silence" (Wittgenstein, 2001, p. 89). He is adapting the injunction from the Sirach, the Book of the old testament divine Joshua ben Sira, cited but not included in the Jewish Liturgy. It appears in the Christian Bible as Ecclesiastes (but is not accepted by all Protestants).

According to the Sirach (3: 21–22):

21 Seek not out things that are too hard for thee, neither search the things that are above thy strength.

22 But what is commanded thee, think thereupon with reverence, for it is not needful for thee to see with thine eyes the things that are in secret.

Ecclesiastes, the Christian biblical form of the Sirah, also declares in verse 22 of the King James translation of 3:21–22: "Wherefore I perceive that *there* is nothing better, than that a man should rejoice in his own works; for that *is* his portion: for who shall bring him to see what shall be after him?"

Ecclesiastes, Sira and their twentieth-century philosophical descendant Wittgenstein alike appear to view the Unknowable as the culminating point of all human endeavor. Three hundred years after al-Farabi his work was studied by the thirteenth-century theologian St Thomas Aquinas, who advocated silence, but not submission, in the face of the Unknowable. He declared there was a place for Revelation—divine or perhaps otherwise—in helping reveal further knowledge, and seeking this revelation was a legitimate human occupation (Hammond, 1947, p. 23). Wittgenstein, however, may be supporting the Sirach's injunction. His respectful relationship with theology is conveyed in the Testament-like structure of his book.

While al-Farabi seeks revelation and guidance from the inaccessible divine, allied to his powers of logic, he has a (to us) very modern tendency not to accept limits to his inquiry. He starts where Wittgenstein stops, and stops where Wittgenstein starts, by contemplating what is unknowable and reasoning forward, using the same declarative style, until we arrive at the World, a process he thought would reveal the ideal structure of a State that most closely reflected the perfection in the First Existent, the First Cause. Whereas another literary and philosophical monument of the Medieval, Dante's *Divine Comedy,* takes us beyond human affairs and up to Paradise, and the "neo-Medievalist" Wittgenstein to the limit of all knowledge itself, al-Farabi rejects Wittgenstein's final injunction to silence and prepares a practical guide to government based on what is produced when trying to comprehend the unknowable, the incomprehensible, the unattainable.

From ultimate perfection to perfectible communication

To understand why Abu Nasr al-Farabi persists in this quest, and his connection to our theme, it is important to place his thinking in his own time, and not our own. A strong Platonic influence is apparent in his attempt to think through what the Ideal implied for governance. His status in the Middle East Islamic World as "the Second Teacher" (after Aristotle) has contributed to ideas of government and by extension to public communication.

Al-Farabi takes unknowable perfection as his starting point, as Alpha rather than Omega. From the First, "the 'thing' which should be believed to be God (Allah)" (al-Farabi, 1985, p. 39) the book descends through the Angels, heavenly bodies, material bodies, matter and form and how they should be described, material natural bodies and their order of rank, the species, the constitution of humanity—soul and body, of male and female, the constitution of the soul, the need to associate and cooperate, and "what the excellent city is; what keeps it together" (al-Farabi, 1985, p. 47), and "what the first excellent ruler ought to be" (al-Farabi, 1985, p. 47).

The author is now able to explain how the ruler is to be prepared for the task, to discuss the "ultimate felicities attained by the souls of the citizens of the excellent cities in the hereafter" (al-Farabi, 1985, p. 49), and to provide accounts of imperfect cities and principles that lead to "wretchedness reached after death" and "erring religions" (al-Farabi, 1985, p. 49). Al-Farabi does not see earthly perfection as the end of the business of civic life and participation. In the virtuous city, the virtuous person "can receive cooperation in exercising the political dimension of its virtue" (Azadpur, 2003, p. 568). The political philosopher and classicist Leo Strauss turned to al-Farabi as a rationalist, logical alternative to an unattractive modern rationalism which he saw "as somehow in the service of the conquest of nature, and, as such, having an essentially practical aim" (Colmo, 1992, p. 966). He believed al-Farabi's less material, more attractive philosophic quest for the ideal life also had a practical, non-theoretical dimension, channelled through a ruler somewhat but not wholly modelled upon the philosopher-kings of Plato's *Republic*. Strauss wrote of Aristotle's *Politics* that: "Man transcends the city only by pursuing true happiness, not by pursuing happiness however understood" (Strauss, 1978, p. 49).

Al-Farabi also seeks the truth, whose source he locates in perfection instead of happiness. We shall see this ideal violently rejected by later authors, who help usher in new communication techniques. After *Analects, The Republic* and *On the Perfect State*, we shall find no more pursuit of collective perfectibility here except Marx and Engels who like al-Farabi equate the achievement of perfection with the obliteration of unfettered communication.

Al-Farabi's conception of perfection flows not from the lives of ancient sages, or the inculcation of values into selected leaders, but from the utter, unblemished, incomprehensible First Existent. "The First does not exist for the sake of anything else" writes al-Farabi (1985, p. 91), yet it brings everything that exists into existence. The First does not need two elements—one being to substantify (give substance to) its "essence"; the other to create or communicate "through which something else comes from it" (al-Farabi, 1985, p. 93). Humans do need communication, which al-Farabi describes as one or more of the two things that define us. "Our substantification is due to one of them, namely thought [or 'speech' logos], but our writing to the other, namely the art of writing" (al-Farabi, 1985, p. 93).

All that comes from the First can be arranged in order of rank, each a little less perfect than the thing before (al-Farabi, 1985, 2.2; p. 95). The First is generous, and "does not neglect any existence beneath its existence" (al-Farabi, 1985, 2.2; p. 95). From the First "emanates the existence of the Second" (al-Farabi, 1985, 3.1; p. 101). From the incorporeal Second, thinking of its own essence and of the First, comes a Third, which "as a result of its substantification in its specific essence" leads to the heavens and the fixed stars (al-Farabi, 1985, 2.2; p. 103), leading to the Fourth, Fifth and so on, until the Eleventh is reached, each substantified as a planet, from Saturn, including the Sun and finally, with the Eleventh existent, our Moon. With the Eleventh Existent, we come upon sublunary existents that need matter "made in such a way that they have their most defective existences in the beginning, and start from it" (al-Farabi, 1985, 4.2; p. 107).

Matter also ascends until it is as perfected as it is possible for it to be. Some forms are natural bodies like fire, air, water, earth, vapour, flame, stones, plants and animals "which lack speech and thought" and animals "which have speech and thought" (al-Farabi, 1985, 4.3; p. 103). "There is nothing after the animal endowed with speech and thought that surpasses it in excellence" (al-Farabi, 1985, 6.1; p. 113). It is a flawed excellence, since apart from the First Existence, differences between the subordinate levels are "contrarieties", and "contrariety is itself a deficiency of existence" (al-Farabi, 1985, 7.10; p. 133).

Overcoming human imperfection with one-way communication

The animal endowed with speech and thought, the human being, is the origin of State communication. According to al-Farabi, the human soul has five faculties. The first is nutrition. The remaining and most important for this theme begin with sense, located in the heart, which rules the five auxiliary senses:

> as if they were carriers of the news, each of whom is charged with a particular genus of news or with news from one province of the realm. The ruling faculty is like the king in whose house the news which the messengers from the provinces have brought is put together.
>
> (al-Farabi, 1985, 10.3; p. 169)

The faculty of representation is also located in the heart (the ruling organ, followed in rank by brain, liver and spleen), controlling the senses ("sensibles") and exercising judgement over them, connecting and separating them in various ways so that "some of the things imagined (or 'represented') by humans agree with those perceived by the senses and others differ from them" (al-Farabi, 1985, 10.4; p. 169). The rational faculty's "rule extends over the other faculties" al-Farabi wrote (perhaps hopefully) (al-Farabi, 1985, 10.5; p. 169); the appetitive faculty "by which desire or dislike of a thing occurs" (al-Farabi, 1985, 10.6; p. 171), manifests itself in the will, and decides whether knowing or doing a thing apprehended by the other senses "ought either to be accepted or rejected" (al-Farabi, 1985, 10.4; p. 169).

The human body imperfectly guides communication, as signals from the First Existent are faint, and presumably, based on al-Farabi's earlier deductions, reserving most of itself for the eternal part of us after bodily destruction has occurred.

The imperfections of communication in al-Farabi's work are magnified by the possibility that he may have disbelieved in the immortal soul, except for the Medieval philosophical idea of an "active intellect" that, in contrast to the receiving "material" or "passive intellect", creates actual knowledge from potential intelligibles in our environment. Certainly, his First Existent is extremely self-contained. Al-Farabi scholar the Reverend Robert Hammond examined his subject's belief in immortality, citing the Spanish Islamic and Aristotelian philosopher Ibn Rushd (often known by his Latinized name of Averroes), who two centuries after *On the Perfect State* quoted al-Farabi as saying: "Man's supreme good in this life is to attain knowledge. But to say that man after death becomes a separate form is an old wives' tale; for whatever is born and dies is incapable of becoming immortal" (Hammond, 1947, p. 37). Hammond himself concludes "it is difficult indeed to tell whether or not Alfarabi [sic] believed in it. Most probably he did not" (Hammond, 1947, p. 37).

The authority of the State is therefore essential to earthly perfection, giving the best possible mortal representatives' power to interpret any signals to them from the non-corporeal existences and intellects above. Al-Farabi takes a lengthy but for him necessary ordering of existences, intellects, senses and organs (down to blood and semen) and reaches its parallel in civic society, a society constructed by humans themselves, but using properties bequeathed by supernatural intellects and entities. What is its purpose? To let us employ our active intellects and carry potential knowledge to the material (bodily) intellect designed to receive and interpret it. To lead us toward "careful examination, deliberation, practical thought and a desire to find out things" (al-Farabi, 1985, 13.4; p. 205), by interpreting potential intelligibles "supplied to him only in order to be used by him to reach his ultimate perfection, i.e. felicity" (al-Farabi, 1985, 13.5; p. 205). Felicity in humanity, and presumably the perfect State, will not need material support, since it has achieved an incorporeal, immaterial state "continuously for ever" (al-Farabi, 1985, 13.5; p. 207):

> Felicity is the good which is pursued for its own sake and it is never at any time pursued for obtaining something else through it, and there is nothing greater beyond it for man to obtain.
>
> (al-Farabi, 1985, 13.6; p. 207)

When felicity remains unknown, the faculties are misdirected and "the actions of man will all be ignoble" (al-Farabi, 1985, 14.1; p. 211).

PR in the perfect State

So despite its imperfect human origins, communication can help us overcome imperfection. It is active intellect, converting potential knowledge to material intellect. It also illuminates material intellect, biologically through the senses, and politically through correctly expressing faith. The media are the senses themselves, and most of the human faculties that give us our identity and potential to reach felicity.

Who must do this communicating? "It is not impossible" that persons exist whose faculty of representation reaches its "utmost perfection" by correctly interpreting what is shown to it. Such a man is key to the perfect State, and "will obtain through the particulars he receives prophecy (supernatural awareness) of present and future events, and through the intelligibles which he receives prophecy of things divine" (al-Farabi, 1985, 14.9; p. 225). In accordance with the ordering of all things, others who only see such things "through a glass, darkly" (1 Corinthians 13. 12) awake or asleep rank below this person, below them are those who only see in sleep "and express their experience in imitating phrases, in allegories, in enigmatic phrases, 'substitutes' and similes" (al-Farabi, 1985, 14.10; p. 225). The members of these two proto-Jungian groups can move from one to the other, as their temperament changes. There are others "bilious, insane and madmen and their like" (al-Farabi, 1985, 14.11; p. 227) whose temperament has been ruined.

To summarize: al-Farabi's best objective for humans is felicity. His key audiences are ranked some way down in the universal order of things: they are divided into those perfected to the maximum extent possible; those with some awareness of felicity; those with less awareness; and those with none at all. How are such people to be governed, and convinced or shown that they are being governed in the right way?

Societies are needed because attaining human perfection requires cooperation to supply the many things we need, and perhaps it is not surprising to learn that al-Farabi ranked perfect societies as he did everything else, in this case by the definitions great, medium, small (al-Farabi, 1985, 15.2; p. 229). A Great society "is the union of all the societies in the inhabitable world" (al-Farabi, 1985, 15.2; p. 229), a medium society is the union of a nation; a small society the union of a city. The ordering is pursued down to the imperfect societies of village, quarter, street and house.

The problem for al-Farabi is to resolve the difficulties of will and choice, and ensure that people cooperate in the pursuit of felicity, beginning in the city and so on until the cooperative effort covers the whole world. The city is the starting point, and still employing reason and logic on the path of higher and lower orders, al-Farabi compares the city to the body and the body's ruling organs, from heart to lower intestine, and talks about performing "the most noble voluntary actions" possible to each rank, until the ignoble ranks are reached (al-Farabi, 1985, 15.5; p. 237). The ruler is the heart, followed by ranks of people who "perform their actions according to the aims" of the people in the previous rank (al-Farabi, 1985, 15.4; p. 233), until the lowest rank is reached, who are served by no one.

The ruler, ruling the city as the heart does the body, "is the most perfect part of the city in his specific qualification and has the best of everything which anybody else shares with him" (al-Farabi, 1985, 15.5; p. 235). We may remember Plato's rulers, isolated from the temptations of the "best of everything".

The prospect painted by al-Farabi reveals differences between the works in these pages. The thinkers—and doers—Mill and Gandhi, argue that free communication is perfection, protection against the tyranny of a majority or a minority, and even provide suggestions for communicating more effectively. Von Hayek explores the misuse of communication by state orthodoxy. Al-Farabi takes a different approach. He sees the prospect of a State so perfect that any communication suggesting otherwise does not need to exist. Versions of this dream appear in Plato's Republic, More's Utopia, and Marx's communist society. Plato and Confucius seek comparatively more moderate ways to manage popular media more closely. Al-Farabi's emphasis on logical ordering and ranking leads him to a conclusion that seems non-contradictable, a city with "well ordered coherent parts" (al-Farabi, 1985, 15.5; p. 237). Perfection sweeps moderation away, in favour of strict top-down communication that instils obedience and keeps all ranks in the city trudging toward the Golgotha of felicity. The example of the ruler is the cause of the city's rise, with voluntary cooperation from the ranks of its inhabitants "and when one part is out of order he provides it with the means to remove its disorder" (al-Farabi, 1985, 15.5; p. 236–37).

What are those means? They are described as "the arts", and needless to say they too are ordered for service in the city, "just as most men are by their very nature born to serve" (al-Farabi, 1985, 15.6; p. 239). The ruler in the excellent city cannot be ruled by any chance art or any other art, for he is the logical outcome of the natural and divine order, with fully developed active and passive intellects, and has moreover developed an "acquired intellect" which lies between them and is more perfect because more separate from matter than its passive counterpart. "When this occurs," we are told: "[I]t is this man who receives Divine Revelation, and God Almighty grants him Revelation through the mediation of the Active Intellect" (al-Farabi, 1985, 15.10; p. 245).

Equipped with such formidable faculties, it is inevitable that "his art must be an art to which all the other arts tend, and for which they strive in all the actions of the excellent city" (al-Farabi, 1985, 15.8; p. 241). The ruler has intellect, the gift of revelation, physical toughness for war, knows of the path to felicity and has the means of communication: "[H]e should be a good orator and able to rouse [other people's] imagination by well chosen words" (al-Farabi, 1985, 15.11; p. 247).

How, where and when should those words be delivered, and purified of doubt and deceit? In the book's two last chapters, 18 and 19, al-Farabi describes the characteristics of ignorant or misguided cities, and it is clear he is concerned with the power of civic communication to deceive, or to misguide. In chapters 15 to 17 he sets out the roles of philosophy and religion, the afterlife, and in Chapter 15 the conditions for "Perfect associations and perfect rulers". A perfect State's communication is inherently without fault. The ruler (at second best five or six rulers, each excellent but lacking the gift and faculties needed for visionary prophecy) should be physically strong, good at understanding and perceiving everything said to him. He should forget almost nothing, be very bright, fond of truth, able to resist physical and financial temptation, just, strong minded and "have a fine diction, his tongue enabling him to explain to perfection all that is in the recess of his mind" (al-Farabi, 1985, 15.12; p. 248–49).

He who succeeds the perfect ruler must be a philosopher, and "good at guiding the people by his speech to fulfil the laws of the first sovereigns as well as those laws which he will have deduced in conformity with their principles after their time" (al-Farabi, 1985, 15.13; p. 253). It is possible to see, then, a place for public communication; a communication between perfect ruler and less perfect people, cleansed as much as it is possible of dialogue; neither collaborative nor cooperative, except in the sense that his audiences cooperate in obeying and agreeing to it. It is consciousness-raising, one-way communication from a divinely perfected version of *The Republic's* philosopher-king. No need to give even an impression of dialogue, except perhaps in small things. If there is misunderstanding, it is the fault or deficiency of the people for not understanding. Their souls might be diseased "and hence do not listen at all to the words of a man who leads them on the right path, teaches them and puts them straight" (al-Farabi, 1985, 16.6; p. 271).

Since most people in cities are not perfected, what does the Perfect Ruler need to tell them? They need to know of the First Existent and its immaterial, celestial and natural subordinates, about the active intellect, about the city's first ruler and "how revelation is brought about" and those who take his place when he is not available, and "then the excellent city and its people and the felicity which their souls ultimately reach" (al-Farabi, 1985, 17.1; p. 279).

Since these messages are beyond the capacity of earthly communication to convey in their fullness, the ruler and his lieutenants must hope they are "impressed on their souls as they really are" or use religion and philosophy to communicate through "affinity and symbolic representation" (al-Farabi, 1985, 17.2; p. 279). The author does not offer an explanation of how this is to be done; there is no ranking or ordering of communication or target audiences for target media as there is of everything else. Walzer, in his translation of *On the Perfect State*, proposes that this means "strict demonstration" among the chosen philosophers and among their followers "the same unquestioning acceptance as those who comply with the commandments of Scripture" (al-Farabi, 1985, Commentary; p. 474). Walzer offers a lengthy commentary on this section of the book, writing that "al-Farabi obviously aimed at educating within the Islamic world a wider philosophical public of this kind" (al-Farabi, 1985, Commentary; p. 475).

If this is the case, it is possible to discern the same strict, formalized, unquestioning absorption of truth by those ranked below from those ranked above. For the rest, they must hope for insight from symbolic representation, that is allegorical interpretation, "which is the outcome of the efforts of poets and prophets" (al-Farabi, 1985, Commentary; p. 475). The mythological and linguistic resources for this effort are limited, Walzer points out, because unlike the polytheist Greeks and Romans "there exists only one felicity as there is only one God and one truth, and philosophy alone provides the key to this knowledge". Learning from the dialogues in Plato, al-Farabi could set the sequence in time, and "by translating it into the easier language of narration ... make the timeless structure of the world understandable and acceptable to the philosophically untrained" (al-Farabi, 1985, Commentary; p. 478). In other works al-Farabi also refers to the Greek ability to "imitate" or "represent" intelligibles analogically by referring to various "sensibles" like darkness, water or air (al-Farabi, 1985, Commentary; p. 479).

Once everyone is persuaded by strict demonstrations or symbolism, al-Farabi asserts there will be no surrender to sophistic fallacies or lack of understanding (al-Farabi, 1985, 17.3; p. 281). Those who identify the flaws in the particular symbols offered to them will be lifted towards higher symbols, and closer to the truth, and possibly even acquire philosophical wisdom. In this sense, the public communication process is ordered for the most to least perfect, and some mobility is possible (al-Farabi, 1985, 17.4; p. 281).

It is evidently the responsibility of the ruler to make available rites and customs that direct his people toward perfection. We learn in Chapter 18 that this must involve piety, to "say that spiritual things exist who govern and oversee every nation"; to "render homage to the god and the spiritual existents", to "pray to them", to "sing to them hymns of praise and reverence" and most of all to "believe" that the pious will be rewarded after death. (al-Farabi, 1985, 18.12; p. 305). Once again, as in the *Analects* and *The Republic* public communication is equated with managing words, lyrics, rites and images, to achieve a perceived virtue that surpasses all the others. Once again we find concern about the power imperfect forms of communication can wield. Al-Farabi identifies and warns against the risk, inherent in all managed public communication in all time, of eventually disbelieving the whole of the symbols and believing that there is no truth at all. The man communicating those symbols might even be an imposter "who is making statements of that kind as hankering after nothing else than a ruling position or some other good like it" (al-Farabi, 1985, 17.6; p. 285).

Confucius and Plato's main differences with al-Farabi's view of communication are political rather than religious. Among al-Farabi's legacies is an intellectual foundation for ruling that the Middle East's Caliphates could follow. They included the "sublime Porte" of the "Eternal State" that was the

Ottoman Empire, which for centuries managed its public communication far more centrally and effectively than its European rivals.

Al-Farabi has been described as one "with a political agenda rather different from that of a solitary, lonely figure intent upon survival" (Frank, 1993, p. 636). *On the Perfect State* is partly a political argument for the obliteration of dialogue and the rise of unconditional, undiluted one-way communication, filtered in an ordered way down the ordered ranks in the city. It is not modern PR of course; it is scarcely even PR as propaganda, because a perfected environment has no need of Plato's noble falsehoods. In its perfected form messages emanate directly from the ruler, while his subjects wait to receive them: passive, uncritical, and ready to learn. There is no obvious participative element equivalent to Confucius' quest for *dao* using ritual, music and personal example at a local level. There is no sense of a free-flowing Socratic symposium, or even a careful selection process for people who will rule their city by managing ritual, myth, poetry, song and the gods themselves.

Nevertheless, managed public communication of a sort has to exist in the perfect State. However much he may or may not have believed in immortality himself, however limited his proposals in comparison to his predecessors in these pages, al-Farabi's rigidly ordered path to felicity constricts creativity and autonomy in human-centered state communication, for the sake of their souls. This was a result of imagining perfection beyond the limits of knowledge, and the mistake was repeated by later states built on utopian creeds. From the tenth century to the present the obliteration of imperfection almost, but not quite, becomes the obliteration of PR itself.

References

al-Farabi, A.-N. (1985) *On the Perfect State.* Translated by R. Walzer. Oxford: Clarendon Press.

Azadpur, M. (2003) "Review of Muhsin S. Mahdi, Alfarabi and the Foundation of Islamic Political Philosophy, 2001." *Speculum*, 78(2): 566–68.

Colmo, C. (1992) "Theory and Practice: Alfarabi's Plato Revisited." *American Political Science Review*, 966–76.

Frank, D. H. (1993) "Review of Politics and Excellence: The Political Philosophy of Alfarabi by Miriam Galston." *Journal of the American Oriental Society*, 113(4): 636–37.

Hammond, R. (1947) *The Philosophy of Alfarabi and its Influence on Medieval Thought.* New York: Hobson Book Press.

Plato (1997) "Laws." In J. M. Cooper and D. S. Hutchinson (eds) *Complete Works.* Indianapolis, IN: Hackett Publishing Company.

Strauss, L. (1978) *The City and Man.* Chicago, IL: University of Chicago Press.

Wittgenstein, L. (2001). *Tractatus Logico-Philosophicus.* Translated by D. F. Pears and B. F. McGuinness. London: Routledge.

5 PR and the subjugation of reason

Martin Luther (1483–1546), *The Ninety-five Theses* (1517)

Harnessing mass emotion

We have arrived at a much less subtle and very public work, arguably written for a much less subtle time, but by a mind as powerful as those in the earlier chapters. Even in the Internet era, we are astonished by the speed of the revolution in European belief, politics, art, music, science and philosophy, the horrors of war and persecution, and the massive eventual reaction, all precipitated or intensified by the thunderclap of Martin Luther's *Ninety-five Theses*.

Europe, and subsequently much of the world, was recast by this mighty act of communication, and, examined as an artefact made for public communication, it seems very modern. The tone, the media it exploited and the content are a violent break from the methodical structures we have already examined. Here is no civilized conversation, courteous questioning or intricate triumph of logic. This is a closely argued outburst of righteous indignation, not aimed at the general nature of government but at a single issue: religious corruption in the Roman Catholic Church, epitomized by the sale of Indulgences guaranteeing less penance in the hereafter.

Ninety-five Theses is firstly about the demolition of clerical abuses, and only afterwards about a positive alternative, albeit one that threatened the Church which Luther the Augustinian friar and university professor at first wished only to reform. Consider too the assertions thrown out by this document, arranged like Biblical verses. This is "shock" public communication, a stronger variant of the declarative style followed by al-Farabi, or later echoed by Wittgenstein. We may also claim that this document comes closer to modern PR, not just from its tone, but because it is very effectively competing with alternative messages and media that formerly were hard to contradict. Lengthy justifications, or courteous justifications after the manner of Confucius or Plato are not in evidence here. In the *Theses* and his later writing "Luther clearly assumes—and often says explicitly—that the true medium from soul to soul is shared passion and the experience that makes it possible" (Haile, 1976, p. 825).

Ninety-five Theses is an assertion, a manifesto, reason condensed into a series of soundbites. It attracted the new printing presses that were also proliferating at that time, which states and super states like the Catholic Church were unable to tame, however effectively or not they had managed the media prescribed by Confucius, Plato and al-Farabi: rites, ceremonies, songs and the ritual calendar. "For this was the great age, not only of Luther's polemical writing, but of the Flugschriften, the short, cheaply produced pamphlets which sought to mediate the church controversies to a wide audience" (Pettegree, 1992, 6).

It was more than that. In the wake of the *Theses*, the older forms of communication management broke down. New rituals, new music, new hymns and new art were created outside of Rome's control. Luther himself wrote many of the hymns now traditional in the Protestant faith. Consider also the intent of the communication: this was a call to people to form their own relationships with God, less mediated by Rome's misuse of "media" like holy relics, and it was helped by the fact that dissenters now had more communication power in their own hands. They not only had the printing press, they were better able to express their thoughts and feelings. They were more literate, they were often freer from monarchical regulation—regulating themselves in rich trading cities or new confederations like the Swiss Cantons. They were independent craftsmen and guild members charging fees for their specialized services, while on the land they were breaking from what we now call serfdom.

Most of all, they were troubled. They were troubled by government and Church corruption, and they were troubled for the sake of their own souls. *Theses* brought such people as these into conflict with authority's managed access to the next world and eventually aroused radical action against traditional political control over this world—although Luther himself did not go as far as that. It was, in short, an event with many characteristics of our own Information Revolution.

Formerly, concerns about religious abuses—if they were expressed at all—fizzled out or were stamped out. Nevertheless, these concerns ultimately exerted a cumulative influence. The usual methods followed included jesting satire from the scholar and essayist Erasmus, poking fun at the sumptuous excesses of princes, adding that "popes, cardinals and bishops have so diligently followed their steps that they've almost got the start of them" (Erasmus, 1511, "popes, cardinals"). There were occasional incoherent, inchoate and doomed outbreaks of political or religious revolt when such views could be voiced more assertively, as the late fourteenth-century Lollard priest John Ball had done in his long-remembered question to rebellious peasants: "when Adam delved and Eve span, who was then the gentleman?" (Dobson, 1970, p. 375). More often than not, though, the prevailing attitude was amused or resigned toleration of the existing system's shortcomings, cheerfully in Chaucer's bawdy tales of wayward Summoners, Friars, Pardoners and other clerical officials in his late fourteenth-century *Canterbury Tales*; or in that despairing resignation shown by nearly all the souls in Hell and Purgatory Dante encountered in his *Divine Comedy*, written in the early fourteenth century, although he placed an Archbishop in the Ninth and worst circle of Hell. Langland's *Piers the Ploughman*, written around the same time as Chaucer's tales, is more indignant when he accuses Pardoners of being in league with parish priests, who controlled the media that mattered, and who "produced a document covered with Bishop's seals, and claimed to have power to absolve all the people from broken fasts and vows of every kind":

> The ignorant folk believed him and were delighted. They came up and knelt to kiss his documents, while he, blinding them with letters of indulgence thrust in their faces, rakes in their rings and jewellery with his roll of parchment!
>
> (Langland, 1975, "There was also a Pardoner")

But what was the point of resisting? Our bodies were after all "worms' meat" (Bradley, 1995, Soul and Body II). Our fates and perhaps souls are beyond our control. This from the Anglo-Saxon poem now known as Resignation: "from the start poverty proved to be my lot upon the earth so that each year—thanks be to God for it all—I have always suffered more heartfelt hardships and dread than there was in other people" (Bradley, 1995, Resignation). In *The Prince* Machiavelli sees peasants or other "common people" as necessary and potentially powerful props for the legitimacy of his Prince. That book was finished in 1513, four years before Luther's theses were nailed to the door. Thomas More's *Utopia* was published in 1516, and shows much greater sensitivity to the sufferings of small folk, dispossessed by enclosure for sheep grazing and other depredations of great lords ("yea and certain abbots, holy men no doubt") and their servants (More, 1992, p. 28). *Utopia's* fictitious character Raphael Hythloday depicts a realm free from such oppressions, and largely controlled by communities of yeoman farmers and skilled craftspeople, with freedom of religion and a communal Prince.

Ninety-five Theses broke the inertia, and the aloof (if sincere) discussion and channelled the discontent. It gave a clear direction, and blew the old resigned complacency to smithereens across northern Europe. Two choices remained. The Faith that sold penances was either to be rebuilt from the foundations, or reduced to its foundations and never rebuilt. In this sense also, Luther was certainly no Confucius, Plato, or al-Farabi. He did not write for State or Church and centrally directed ritual had no place at all in his own communication, in his plans for the Faith, and in the spiritual struggles of Believers. Luther is the forerunner of a vast loss of patience with the ways organizations worked. In this way, too, his communication is very modern.

Modern PR is also apparent in the mechanics of Luther's approach—in the manifesto style, also so far from Confucius, Plato and al-Farabi. Then there were the famous means of distribution, firstly nailing his work to the door of Wittenberg Cathedral in eastern Germany—he belonged to the local Augustinian monastery—where people concentrate to enter and exit: it would be surprising if he was the only person who did this. Second, it was printed *en masse*; certainly a departure from scholarly manuscripts circulated among a privileged few. Nor was it mere popular pamphleteering—which was known by that time. Luther was a scholar and his words were in Latin, which was only known to a few, but compensated for by the choice of a Cathedral, the main centre of civic worship, whose congregation and officials would include influential and thoughtful persons and readers of Latin—opinion leaders likely to translate, print and spread the word. There was the advantage of being in a city where educated persons interested in ideas were concentrated, and able to discuss and organize their thoughts and themselves. John Ball agitated among peasants: large in number but scattered, illiterate and hard to fuse together into a coherent force. Luther took advantage of the city's new university, its specialized professions and trades, and its civic leadership, and tapped a disturbing, impatient, dynamic, pent-up and concentrated discontent among burgers who knew their own worth. His work fitted the new communication environment that was emerging. The *Theses* were perceived not to be about arming Church and State with new policies, but about arming people with ideas and arousing popular emotion to trigger change. The approach is redolent of German playwright Bertolt Brecht's twentieth-century *Lehrstücke* or learning plays, whose purpose was, first, to make the people aware that they were being oppressed; second, to show them who their oppressors were; third, to explain the steps they must take to deal with the problem. Brecht was a Communist, but the technique was Luther's also.

The effect of this simple method undoubtedly went further than Brecht and perhaps Luther himself anticipated. The *Ninety-five Theses* triggered the Protestant Reformation: a genuine mass movement, international and violently radical. It not only unleashed conflict. It forced into the open a new view of government and God's intentions that caused many people on both sides of the argument to examine themselves and their society more closely, and it finally pushed Catholicism into a brilliant series of reforms and re-examinations known as the Counter-Reformation.

Writing from our own time, this work is interesting because we can see the strong, turbulent intellect and personality behind it. It is the embodiment of a man who on the strength of it became a popular celebrity in his own right—so far as such persons existed in the sixteenth century. Some of the characteristics of celebrity status are obvious: the monuments to him, the paintings and prints of Luther at every stage of his life, and popular interest in his wife and parents; the preservation of places he lived and worked; the collection and publication of his words including casual ones; the continuing popularity of his hymns and catechisms, and the continuing use of his last name as a first or second name. Luther was celebrated by those toiling, troubled, "common people" Confucius spoke of; something that did not happen to Confucius to the same extent for many years; and did not apparently happen to Plato or al-Farabi at all. To a great extent, Luther metamorphosed into one of the rulers al-Farabi spoke of, viewed almost as a Prophet across much of Germany and elsewhere. Far more than Marx, but no more than Gandhi or Confucius—the other three thinkers here who achieved similar status—Luther aroused wide-spread popular adulation that to some extent continues into the present. Needless to say, he also aroused hatred, which was also amply conveyed by the media of the time.

The birth of issues management

Many of Luther's later activities were concerned with setting bounds and order to the changes his works had made, and with restoring authority to its proper sphere. Some of his later writings also reflected, incited and energized the anti-semitism of his time, contributing to its long, tragic and all-too well-known legacy. The *Ninety-five Theses* and its proposals are intimately connected to these issues as well. Nevertheless it is its iconoclasm that matters for managed public communication. With this work, driven into a door, a storm broke which has still not subsided, and has been fed by the communication it released. It is the most significant forerunner of single-issue, campaign-based communication: direct, morally certain, and using passion to energize or distort reason. The titles of some of Luther's later letters, sermons, chapters and books show this tendency: *Babylonian Captivity of the Church* (1520); *The Three Walls of the Romanists* (1520); *Concerning Christian Liberty* (1526); *Internal Warfare of the Child of God* (1535). Furey comments: "Luther used insults to scrub away centuries of detritus. The brush that he and other Protestants used was stiff and punishing, but they applied it eagerly to render transparent the truth of salvation by faith alone" (Furey, 2005, p. 472).

That approach, though, was not wholly Luther's intention in 1517. He wanted the *Ninety-five Theses* to be a "Disputation" subjected to reasoned debate, to test the truth of them. The preamble to the Disputation announced that the theses were to be "discussed at Wittenberg, under the presidency of the Reverend Father Martin Luther" who "also requests that those who are unable to be present and debate orally with us, may do so by letter" (Luther, 2008, Preamble).

A debate took place, once the distractions of heated words and clashing arms are tuned out, but it was limited. The Church was unwilling to discuss and in the eyes of many Germans preferred simply to silence and threaten. It was emotion though, not scholarly disputation, that drove the movement and its opponents; their passion for Faith, hatred for their opponents, and search for God sustained the opposing forces through generations of conflict, more or less coming to an end with the Treaty of Westphalia in 1648, which solidified the idea of national boundaries rather than dynastic identities. Behind them were populations who could in time be alerted to a new identity based on nation-state, or race, or their rights as citizens, rather than region, ruler or religion.

It was said earlier that the *Ninety-five Theses* is concerned with a lengthy attack on an abuse and not—at first—with the construction of a positive alternative. Luther's audiences are all mortal, but he wrote for those in especial fear of death, judgement and damnation. Luther wants their popular opinion to influence the Pope and the clergy. This priority is important, because it further converts his communication into a public campaign, and into all the tools and techniques such a campaign must employ. Luther was not solely interested in expressing his thoughts to a Symposium or a small group of devotees. His words went beyond circles of intellectuals, or still smaller circles of rulers, though later publications were intended specifically for them.

This order of priority is clear in Luther's diagnosis of the situation, and in his slightly less well-known heading for the *Theses* "Disputation of Doctor Martin Luther on the Power and Efficacy of Indulgences". It raises his complaint: how the Church exploits an absolute communication monopoly—over all people concerned about what kind of hereafter they will enjoy or suffer. This monopoly to Luther was an abuse of God and humanity alike. "Ignorant and wicked are the doings of those priests who, in the case of the dying, reserve canonical sentences for purgatory" (Luther, 2008, 10). The media include "Indulgencies", encouraging money payments as canonical (that is, according to set church rules) penalties for sin, which was now converted from a spiritual to a revenue tool, preying upon people in mortal fear. Church penalties should not be presented as a bill in return for fewer days in purgatory, but to set the terms of true contrition. "In former times the canonical penalties were imposed not after, but before absolution, as tests of true contrition" (Luther, 2008, 12). Penitential canons should not be imposed on the dying, who are facing God-given rewards or penalties."The dying are freed by death from all penalties; they are already dead to canonical rules, and have a right to be released from them" (Luther, 2008, 13).

The tool of penalties exploits the most primal of human emotions—the final terror of death, and using the Pope's authority as justification means "that the greater part of the people are deceived by that indiscriminate and high-sounding promise of release from penalty" (Luther, 2008, 24). Luther's objections, the media platform of the *Theses*, and his chosen audience had consequences similar to those we are witnessing today. They would upend all the existing management of public media: of literacy and literature, visual art, law, architecture, ritual and the calendar, even the traditional language of the Bible, and new hands and minds would reshape them. New alternatives would be introduced in all these areas, and create new legitimacies by building a new and (in many regions) more accessible and collaborative communication environment.

Luther as an Augustinian monk tried tempering his attack by attempting to separate the cause and management of the crisis (Indulgencies) from the head of the institution (the Papacy). An "indulgence" originally remitted earthly punishment for sins that had been forgiven. By Luther's time, the procedure was often corrupted into setting the amount of time a soul might be remitted from the halfway house of Purgatory, the realm where lesser sinners went to be purified before entering Paradise. The soul's mortal owner might secure such dubious indulgences by purchasing letters of pardon for particular sins, to an amount prescribed by Canonical (Church Law) judgement, which was delivered by clerical officials.

Luther declared that unscrupulous clergy were misinterpreting the original intention: "by 'full remission of all penalties' the pope means not actually "of all", but only of those imposed by himself" (Luther, 2008, 20). The Church was not trying to rule over the hereafter, only over its own earthly canon: it was this that had been misinterpreted. The *Theses* were an appeal to the Pope to put things right. A year later, Luther went further and dedicated all his writings to the Pope, not seeking at that point to destroy the Church to which he belonged: "Christians are to be taught that the pope, in granting pardons, needs and therefore desires, their devout prayer for him more than the money they bring!" (Luther, 2008, 48).

If the Pope knew of the abuses of pardon-preachers, "he would rather that St Peter's church should go to ashes, than that it should be built up with the skin, flesh and bones of his sheep" (Luther, 2008, 50). Since Pope Leo X was seeking revenue to build a new St Peter's, this assertion was perhaps less apparent to the laity, and certainly unwelcome to his Holiness. Devaluing pardons devalued the media that created demand for them: relics, images, reliquaries and many of the rituals surrounding them. Luther himself said:

> [I]f pardons, which are a very small thing, are celebrated with one bell, with single procession and ceremonies, then the Gospel, which is the very greatest thing, should be preached with a hundred bells, a hundred processions, a hundred ceremonies.
>
> (Luther, 2008, 55)

It was true that popes had from time to time joined those inveighing against the abuse of indulgences, but Pope Leo X could not brook such powerfully expressed doubts about his divine rights, and its impact on the Church's revenue stream. The *Theses* cut too deeply into Catholicism's spiritual and earthly authority. In parenthesis, we shall see this mistake being made elsewhere. Gandhi also did not in his autobiography—as we shall see— seek to leave the British Empire, and said as much, but once again the authorities were unable to respond imaginatively, and once again, as with Luther, they were eventually swept aside by the communication power of a great man and the social forces they had galvanized.

Nor did Luther aim at upending the social structure, although his arguments presaged a more equal relationship between priest and laity. Much like Plato, Confucius and al-Farabi: "Luther's city is a domain of peace and order, not a realm where citizens live in a community and are supposed to be politically active, participating in government" (Rublack, 1985, p. 19).

Again, though, the force of his own communication swept his restraint aside. The city, which once again is seen as the dynamo of the *polis*, was already a powerful factor in Europe. Many were already largely self-governing, building their own identities and traditions, attracting the ambitious and independent-minded, and valued by rulers for their revenue and amenities. The *Theses* accelerated this by questioning the spiritual links between civic and religious authority: "To say that the cross, emblazoned with the papal arms, which is set up [by the preachers of Indulgencies], is of equal worth with the Cross of Christ, is blasphemy" (Luther, 2008, 79). "The bishops, curates and theologians who allow such talk to be spread among the people, will have an account to render" (Luther, 2008, 80).

Time and again, Luther attacks the credibility of religious authority's commonly used communication medium, the letter of pardon. "They will be condemned eternally, together with their teachers, who believe themselves sure of their salvation because they have letters of pardon" (Luther, 2008, 32). "Every truly repentant Christian has a right to full remission of penalty and guilt, even without letters of pardon" (Luther, 2008, 36). "It is most difficult, even for the very keenest theologians, at one and the same time to commend to the people the abundance of pardons and [the need of] true contrition" (Luther, 2008, 39). And ultimately: "The assurance of salvation by letters of pardon is vain, even though the commissary, nay, even though the pope himself, were to stake his soul upon it" (Luther, 2008, 52).

Luther galvanized long-held doubts, and concentrated them on his person. Two sides were identified: the oppressor and the oppressed—one believing and the other disbelieving in Pardons. On the former side were those whose livelihoods Luther threatened: a large audience of lay people and clerical officials. Their fortunes rested on a popular belief in power of their visible, tangible media. It was this Luther questioned, offering instead the prospect of a more personal relationship with God written and spoken in the language of the people themselves, with less need for middlemen.

The relics, images and other communication materials Luther discredited, furthermore, were often where the majority of people regularly encountered God—the images they hung round their shoulders, or pinned to their clothing, or put on their fingers; the feast days where precious relics were publicly paraded, the promise of relief from purgatory in exchange for a purchased document few of them could read. His attack on such intimate artefacts inevitably aroused a sustained reaction using public communication and force of arms.

Anger management

Luther employs other powerful methods still used by effective issues management: repetition, directness, brevity, certainty and simplicity. Nine theses of the ten from numbers forty-two and fifty-one begin with "Christians are to be taught" (in the original Latin, "Docendi sunt christiani"), for instance, and each of the nine, and others, get to the point with a directness, brevity and simplicity that is perhaps rare when an academic puts pen to paper. See the English translation of thesis forty-seven or instance: "Christians are to be

taught that the buying of pardons is a matter of free will, and not of com-
mandment" (Luther, 2008, 47). Another technique was repeated assertive
questioning, which Luther presented as "the shrewd questionings of the
laity" (Luther, 2008, 80). Eight of the ninety-five theses (from eighty-two to
eighty-nine inclusive) are thus presented consecutively, with a strong effect.
For example "Since the pope, by his pardons, seeks the salvation of souls
rather than money, why does he suspend the indulgences and pardons
granted heretofore, since these have equal efficacy?" (Luther, 2008, 89). Luther
ends the row of questions with an assertion: "To repress these arguments and
scruples of the laity by force alone, and not to resolve them by giving reasons,
is to expose the Church and the pope to the ridicule of their enemies, and to
make Christians unhappy" (Luther, 2008, 90). Assertiveness is also conveyed in the three theses beginning "We say", to counter opposing arguments,
as in: "We say, on the contrary, that the papal pardons are not able to
remove the very least of venial sins, so far as its guilt is concerned"
(Luther, 2008, 76).

Finally, there is a "They"—another side, a side described with enough lack
of clarity for Luther's supporters to decide for themselves who "They" might
be. "They" are, in general, numbered among the bishops, clergy and particularly priestly pardoners: persons in error who get between people and Pope,
and corrupt the Faith by selling specious pardons, and—most disturbingly of
all for the purchasers—those who believe pardons do any good. These
"They" "will be condemned eternally, together with their teachers" (Luther,
2008, 32); "preach no Christian doctrine" (Luther, 2008, 35); "are enemies of
Christ and of the pope, who bid the Word of God be altogether silent in some
Churches, in order that pardons may be preached in others" (Luther, 2008,
53); "now fish for the riches of men" (Luther, 2008, 66); "allow a man who is
impious and their enemy to buy out of purgatory the pious soul of a friend of
God" (Luther, 2008, 84).

Then there is the "Us", the common people, the laity referred to earlier
who are misled into purchasing a relationship with God via pardons, instead
of seeking Him by searching their own conscience. The common people
appearing in the *Analects, The Republic* and *On the Perfect State* are objects
for discussion, analysis and management. Luther takes another approach: he
places himself alongside them, and puts their concerns at the heart of his case,
because their souls are in danger. The people "are deceived by that indiscriminate and high-sounding promise of release from penalty" (Luther, 2008,
24); must not "falsely think" pardons are "preferable to other good works of
love" (Luther, 2008, 41); are not told enough about the "'treasures of the
Church,' out of which the pope grants indulgences" (Luther, 2008, 56);
wrongly "believe themselves sure of their salvation because they have letters
of pardon" (Luther, 2008, 32); "are bound to keep back what is necessary for
their own families, and by no means to squander it on pardons" (Luther,
2008, 46). In Furey's words "his cause thus thrived upon opposition" (Furey,
2005, p. 476).

Here is another of the common threads in all issues management, an allegation of misusing precious resources. Luther condemned the misuse of faith and ritual, and of money. Money is "cajoled" from people by "hawkers of pardons" (Luther, 2008, 51); people are led to think "souls fly out of purgatory" when in fact "gain and avarice" are increased "when the penny jingles into the money box" (Luther, 2008, 27 and 28). Why is the pope not using his own money to build St Peter, "rather than the money of poor believers" (Luther, 2008, 86)? Faith and ritual are compromised because as mentioned earlier some churches are shut down when indulgences are preached in others. True contrition is compromised by misuse of prayer and ritual. This recalls Confucius' wish to re-establish them as guides to virtue, but Luther wants to re-establish them by taking drastic action against authority, which Confucius would not have welcomed. Luther's radical approach was influenced by the concept of individual repentance, and the need for individuals to pursue it, and to wrestle with their demons in order to save their souls: "True contrition" "seeks and loves penalties" (Luther, 2008, 40); no one can be "sure that his own contrition is sincere" (Luther, 2008, 30).

Brevity, direct and powerful language, assertions, direct questions, repetition, simplicity, a clear choice for or against choice, with the wrong side presented as bad—and in Luther's case, blasphemous. A strong popular relationship to mass audiences is being created, and carried across Europe by printing, word of mouth and transportation routes. It contains all the essentials of campaign management, including a ringing conclusion in theses ninety-two and ninety-three, an *Aux armes, citoyens,* at least *armes spirituelles*, that is a simple, universal, dramatic synthesis and which in the English translation requires exclamation marks and resembles the "WORKING MEN OF ALL COUNTRIES, UNITE! At the end of Marx and Engel's *Communist Manifesto* (Marx and Engels, 1998, p. 77).

> 92 Away then, with all those prophets who say to the people of Christ, "Peace, peace," and there is no peace!
>
> (Luther, 2008, 92)

> 93 Blessed be all those prophets who say to the people of Christ, "Cross, cross," and there is no cross!
>
> (Luther, 2008, 93)

Finally, Luther presents his alternative, to be "diligent in following Christ" (Luther, 2008, 94) for themselves, and to "be confident of entering heaven through many tribulations" (Luther, 2008, 95). This was the possibility: a liberated relationship with God unmediated by corrupt or distant middlemen.

Luther's issues communication had the added benefit of being first. It appeared at the dawn of the information revolution made by printing, and catalysed it by helping to increase literacy: "The common man, always curious, wanted to know what the fuss was all about. That he could indeed find out and understand for himself was after all a major argument of Luther's theology (Haile, 1976, p. 817).

As with some organizations exposed to intense public criticism from today's public critics, private leakers and whistle-blowers, the sixteenth-century Church's first responses were defensive, authoritarian, proscriptive and threatening, and finally violent—as indeed were their opponents. The idea of a new response, a communicated response to hearts and minds using media differently had to be learned, and was eventually most effectively conveyed in the Counter-Reformation, which got underway in the mid-sixteenth century. It recognized that the people Luther activated were a force for communication needing a response more reminiscent of the conciliatory and flexible approaches adopted by the Church a thousand years before, for the conversion of northern Europe. It was also the recognition that a powerful new means of public communication had spread across the continent, and later elsewhere, and that this affected the more orderly structure of managed communication that had preceded it, and in some cases discredited it altogether. The tone of Luther's communication took the *Ninety-five Theses* beyond the realm of religion. His impact and that of his followers is visible in secular public relations today, particularly in non-profit campaigns and issues management. As Constance Furey notes "The scathing insults that fill texts by Christian reformers can shock even a jaded modern reader" (Furey, 2005, p. 469). There have been unexpected and ironic communication outcomes. Luther's separation of Church from State authority, and his popular appeal, presented the decidedly atheist East German Government with an opportunity to cooperate with the country's powerful Lutheran church, revise their official attitude toward Luther, give an impression of tolerance, encourage national feeling, and attract foreign tourists and currency by declaring 1983 Luther Year (Goeckel, 1984).

Yet Luther's main communication legacy is surely to unlock its dynamism and turbulence. He raised violent new possibilities for the evolving craft of managed public communication. Along with his predecessors in these pages, he placed reason at the heart of his argument, but his inflammatory style could not be restrained. "It was not a pope who decreed dispensations from vows could be granted" he later wrote, "but an ass changed for a pope, that made this decretal; so egregiously senseless and godless is it" (Luther, 1520, The Sacrament of Baptism).

Across Europe monks deserted their cloisters, holy rites were mocked, churches commandeered by evangelicals, preachers publicly criticised, and liberty of worship spread, but not always tolerance of other forms of worship. Finally, Europe and especially Germany stumbled into armed conflict, sporadic at first, but growing into the horrors of the Thirty Years War (1618–48) described by Dame Veronica Wedgewood in 1934 as "the outstanding example in European history of meaningless conflict" (Wedgwood, 1989, p. 526). Luther's fury could not be constrained, not by the Church, or by Luther himself. The kind of communication he encouraged tore reason from his hands and turned it into gunpowder.

References

Bradley, S. A. J. (1995) *Anglo-Saxon Poetry.* London: Dent.

Dobson, R. B. (1970) *The Peasants' Revolt of 1381.* London: Macmillan.

Erasmus, D. (1511) *The Praise of Folly.* Public Domain.

Furey, C. (2005) "Invective and Discernment in Martin Luther, D. Erasmus, and Thomas More." *Harvard Theological Review,* 98(4): 469–88.

Goeckel, R. F. (1984) "The Luther Anniversary in East Germany." *World Politics,* 37 (1): 112–33.

Haile, H. G. (1976) "Luther and Literacy." *Publications of the Modern Language Association of America,* 91(5): 816–28.

Langland, W. (1975). *Piers the Ploughman.* Translated by J. F. Goodrich. Harmondsworth: Penguin Books.

Luther, M. (2008) *The Ninety-five Theses on the Power and Efficacy of Indulgences. (95 Theses).* Salt Lake City, UT: Project Gutenberg.

——(1520) *The Babylonian Captivity of the Church.* Retrieved from www.lutherdansk. dk/Web-Babylonian%20Captivitate/Martin%20Luther.htm.

Pettegree, A. (1992) *The Early Reformation in Europe.* Cambridge: Cambridge University Press.

Rublack, H. C. (1985) "Martin Luther and the Urban Social Experience." *The Sixteenth Century Journal,* 16(1): 15–32.

Marx, K. and Engels, F. (1998) *The Communist Manifesto: A Modern Edition.* With an introduction by E. J. Hobsbawm. London: Verso.

More, T. (1992) *Utopia.* New York: W. W. Norton & Company.

Wedgwood, C. V. (1989) *The Thirty Years War.* London: Routledge.

6 Willpower and the expansion of PR

Carl von Clausewitz (1780–1831),
On War (1832–35)

The military foundations of communication management

Luther triggered the Reformation, the Reformation ignited the Thirty Years War, the Thirty Years War ended with the Treaty of Westphalia and the rise of nation-states, and the nation-state led to revolution, wars of conquest, nationalist reaction and Carl von Clausewitz. *On War* is a big book, and its breadth and main subject have had many implications for public relations, so a preamble is needed here.

In *On War*, Clausewitz exposed new forces that needed managed public communication. He did so on behalf of the established State, against others who used communication to make a revolutionary State. After his death from cholera in 1831, his wife and a group of officers between 1832 and 1835 published the work in eight volumes as Clausewitz had intended. The first volume was more or less complete, and the remaining seven arranged from the papers he had left.

On War was not an immediate success. It became required reading for Prussian, and later German officers, after it was heavily praised by Helmuth von Moltke the Elder (1800–891), for thirty years Chief of the Prussian and later German General Staff. Officers of the Japanese Imperial Army became familiar with the book while training in Germany in the 1880s, and several Japanese translations appeared which influenced an army already much-guided by German military practices (Oki, 2011). By the late nineteenth century *On War* enjoyed massive political influence in an age of industrial and imperial expansion, much as did its maritime counterpart written in 1890, Mahan's *The Influence of Sea Power upon History, 1660–1783*. It was a period when technological and social change produced deep reflections on military doctrine, and in particular its relationship to civil society and politics. Today, for this reason alone, *On War* was not confined to military audiences, though today's American Army also professes to pursue Clausewitzian principles. Non-military students of Clausewitz included Lenin, who studied him at length and cited him in his writings, including the brochure "Socialism and War", where he considered Clausewitz's most famous dictum that "War is merely the continuation of policy by other means". Clausewitz himself had written vividly on that subject, saying: "Politics is the womb in which war develops" (Clausewitz, 1993, p. 173).

And more prosaically on the consequences: "The political object is the goal, war is the means of reaching it, and means can never be considered in isolation from their purpose" (Clausewitz, 1993, p. 99)

Lenin responded: "Marx always rightly considered this position the theoretical basis of views on the significance of each given war. Marx and Engels always looked at individual wars exactly from this point of view" (Davis and Kohn, 1977, p. 193).

The influence of *On War* on the Soviet Union's first leader, on the German and Japanese armies and societies, and latterly on the US Army—and possibly society—is enough to merit inclusion here, quite apart from its impact elsewhere. Why? Because Clausewitz took elements needed and exploited by strategic communication, and placed them at the heart of his doctrine. In doing so, he helped change the relationship of the State to its subjects, in ways even he could not anticipate, as his later adherents mediated the communication between the two.

A reason for Clausewitz's inability to avoid communication lies in his own experience, and his view that the role of politics in war had been changed in his lifetime. In the late seventeenth and most of the eighteenth centuries "the only influence the people continued to exert on war was an indirect one—through its general virtues or shortcomings" (Clausewitz, 1993, Book Eight, p. 712). War was left to standing professional armies paid from the State treasury (Clausewitz, 1993, Book Eight, p. 713).

Behind their fortresses and positions, hedged in further by intricate dynastic relationships between states, Clausewitz believed armies "came to form a state within a state, in which violence gradually faded away" (Clausewitz, 1993, Book Eight, p. 712), and the greatest of generals like Frederick the Great or Gustavus Aldophus had to be content with limited successes (Clausewitz, 1993, Book Eight, p. 714). At the end of the eighteenth century, a war-making State—as in the days of the "Tartars", and "the republics of antiquity" (Clausewitz, 1993, Book Eight, p. 712)—suddenly needed its people as part of the war effort once again. In Revolutionary France "war again became the business of the people—a people of thirty millions" who now were citizens, not subjects and "instead of governments and armies as heretofore, the full weight of the nation was thrown into the balance" (Clausewitz, 1993, Book Eight, pp. 715–16), waging war on a vaster scale that France's opponents were initially unable to equal (Clausewitz, 1993, Book Eight, p. 716).

Clausewitz witnessed French citizen armies defeating time and again the professional armies of kings and emperors. In a short time, war was suddenly "a concern of the people" (Clausewitz, 1993, Book Eight, p. 716) of Spain, Russia, Austria, the German states and Prussia, expanding the size of their armies, their theatre of operations, and the stakes involved. The people were now involved and "War, untrammeled by any conventional restraints," Clausewitz wrote "had broken loose in all its elemental fury" (Clausewitz, 1993,

Book Eight, p. 717). Clearly, professional training was not enough: will and common purpose, hostile feelings between entire nations would be essential in future warfare, and that too meant adding a socio-political perspective to military operations:

> Theorists are apt to look on fighting in the abstract as a trial of strength without emotion entering into it. This is one of a thousand errors which they quite consciously commit because they have no idea of the implications.
>
> (Clausewitz, 1993, Book Two, p. 159)

"Modern wars are seldom fought without hatred between nations;" Clausewitz noted in Book Two, "this serves more or less as a substitute for hatred between individuals" (Clausewitz, 1993, Book Two, p. 159). The "patriotic spirit" of "national feeling"—defined as "enthusiasm, fanatical zeal, faith and general temper"—of the troops was one of war's four "Principal Moral Elements" (Clausewitz, 1993, Book Three, p. 218).

The editor of *On War*'s 1909 English edition, using Colonel J. J. Graham's first full translation in 1874, saw danger in the part states were playing in developing trade. "War between great nations is only a question of time. No Hague Conferences can avert it" (Clausewitz and Maguire, 1909, "War between great nations"). Clausewitz viewed patriotic emotions as a vital asset, but also a necessary constraint, for subordination to state policy was the only way to "subject to reason" the "blind natural force" and "paradoxical trinity" of "primordial violence, hatred and enmity" required in war (Clausewitz, 1993, Book One, p. 101). A fully autonomous war cannot be thought of (Clausewitz, 1993, Book One, p. 101). It would be waged without the reason or restraint imposed by politics. Like Machiavelli in *The Prince* (1513), Clausewitz wrote about the world as it was, not as it should be, after the manner of Plato and al-Farabi.

A final reason for Clausewitz's impact on society and communication, aside from the war/policy relationship, was his idea about war's dual nature. In the words of Peter Paret, an editor of the 1993 Everyman edition of *On War*, Clausewitz envisaged two kinds of conflict, depending on the purpose behind them; "war waged with the aim of completely defeating the enemy"—to destroy it or force it to accept any terms offered; and war over specific territory either to retain it as a conquest or use it as a bargaining chip in peace talks (Clausewitz, 1993, Book One, p. 24). These approaches involved practical tactical and strategical knowledge, and differing degrees of intangibles: will, leadership, perseverance, public opinion, "the temper of the population of the theater of war" (Clausewitz, 1993, Book Three, p. 216), passion and others to be examined here. For now it is enough to remember that Clausewitz often collectively described them in Chapter Three of Book Two as "moral":

> [T]he moral elements are among the most important in war. They constitute the spirit that permeates war as a whole, and at an early stage they

establish a close affinity with the will that moves and leads the whole mass of force, practically merging with it, since the will is itself a moral quantity.

(Clausewitz, 1993, p. 216)

"Unfortunately" Clausewitz continues "they will not yield to academic wisdom" (Clausewitz, 1993, p. 216), yet "History provides the strongest proof of the importance of moral factors" (Clausewitz, 1993, p. 217). Clausewitz chose to examine the subject "in an incomplete and impressionistic manner" (Clausewitz, 1993, p. 217), "to have indicated the spirit in which the argument of this book was conceived" (Clausewitz, 1993, p. 217). That may have been the intention, but he (and his later editors) returns to the subject again and again in all eight volumes. Moral factors pepper the work, and in part as opportunities and problems of perception, because war has political origins and political objectives, and an army must throw down its enemy's moral force, inseparable from its material strength (Clausewitz, 1993, p. 157).

The enemy's effort must be overcome by invasion, by operations that increase the enemy's suffering, and most importantly by wearing them down (Clausewitz, 1993, Book One, p. 106) by gradual erosion of the enemy's physical and moral power to resist (Clausewitz, 1993, Book One, p. 101). "Even a modest victory" may begin the process like an "electric charge" to the losing nation's nervous system, creating hesitation, dejection and resignation (Clausewitz, 1993, Book Four, p. 303).

The last point of this preamble is to remind ourselves how such a carefully structured, and closely reasoned work as *On War* is itself a crucible for the turbulent emotional forces discussed here, and how it mirrors the Romantic period that brought the cooler rationalizations of the Enlightenment to a close. It is unlikely Clausewitz would have been bothered by that: his work was a powerful alternative to the technical, mathematical, even geometrical approach of his predecessors, the most well-known of whom was General Antoine-Henri Jomini, a Swiss who had served the French and (like Clausewitz), the Russians. Clausewitz's approach admitted and welcomed political turbulence, chance, the moral factors mentioned earlier, particularly in the first four books, in which many of his general principles were set down. Perhaps a little like al-Farabi, he carefully structures his book from the general to the specific, or as he put it, from "simple to complex" (Clausewitz, 1993, Book One, p. 83).

In many ways Clausewitz embraced Romanticism, using its energy to reject or invigorate many technical and highly quantitative approaches to his subject. One cannot imagine the strategists of Europe's *anciens régimes* in the first half of the eighteenth century, not even those in the Thirty Years War, writing these reflections, more sympathetic to Beethoven or Byron than to traditional views of command: "Parenthetically, it should be noted that the seeds of wisdom that are to bear fruit in the intellect are sown less by critical studies and learned monographs than by insights, broad impressions and flashes of intuition" (Clausewitz, 1993, p. 217).

There could be no more of the older "spurious philosophy" that a battle could end once honour had been satisfied (Clausewitz, 1993, Book Four, p. 315). Clausewitz took the Romantic era on behalf of the State and gave its passionate intensity direction, shape, purpose, and what has often proved to be a terrible integrity.

What communication is not in *On War*

This is a parenthesis, but one that must be inserted here if we are to understand how Clausewitz understood the relationship between moral factors (or willpower), warfare and communication. "The commander-in-chief need not be a learned historian or a pundit" ("publicist" in the 1909 edition) (Clausewitz, 1993, Book Two, p. 169), Clausewitz wrote, but "he must know the character, the habits of thought and action, and the special virtues and defects" of his troops—he need not seek personal publicity, but must have insight into people as well as his technical knowledge. Understanding his soldiers gives him the ability to control the moral forces that determine their effectiveness.

Commanders have been pundits, or publicists, before and after Clausewitz. Julius Caesar wrote books on his military campaigns. Napoleon publicized himself to the French Army and Europe. Some of the battles the allies fought in the Second World War were publicity battles between themselves: for instance General Alexander (UK) versus General Clark (USA) in Italy. Montgomery, Patton and MacArthur cultivated the media, their armies and nations, often with their own PR teams. The connection between self-publicity and the emphasis on moral factors seems on the face of it to have escaped Clausewitz.

Arousing the will

In *On War*, will and "moral factors" are the reasons for communication, and these shall be explored here, starting with the role of will. To begin with, Clausewitz defined war as "an act of force to compel the enemy to do our will" (Clausewitz, 1993, Book One, p. 83). Willpower and steadfastness will allow warfare to reach its objective (Clausewitz, 1993, Book Three, p. 226).

Today this sort of language is more familiar to us. In Clausewitz's day it represented fresh thinking about human relationships to art, nature, each other, and war. It is the product of revolution and Romanticism, forces that Clausewitz harnessed to his theories, a "great willpower which yields only reluctantly" (Clausewitz, 1993, Book Three, p. 238). Willpower is a factor in deciding the impact of a military decision in a state of tension, and "resembles the explosion of a carefully sealed mine" (Clausewitz, 1993, Book Three, p. 261).

The successes of France, of Russia in resisting invasion, and the national spirit of resistance aroused in Prussia by Napoleonic domination demonstrated willpower's potency, and its strengthening attachment to national feeling. Governments would be foolish not to use this resource (Clausewitz, 1993, Book Three, p. 258).

In this new warfare, national perceptions must be coordinated: "The passions that are to be kindled in war must already be inherent in the people" (Clausewitz, 1993, Book One, p. 101). Will is what directs those passions behind a war's political motive (or object). Political objectives "can elicit *differing* reactions from different peoples, and even from the same people at different times. We can therefore take the political object as a standard only if we think of the influence it can exert upon the forces it is meant to move" (Clausewitz, 1993, Book One, p. 90). The smaller your objective, the less passion, politics and will is required by either side. At the other extreme "the more powerful and inspiring the motives for war, the more they affect the belligerent nations and the fiercer the tensions" (Clausewitz, 1993, Book One, p. 99).

The collision of wills, therefore, was an essential ingredient of modern warfare. Our effort and the enemy's power of resistance is "the product of two inseparable factors, viz, *the total means at his disposal and the strength of his will*" (Clausewitz, 1993, Book One, p. 86). The goal is to end the war by "paralysis of the enemy's forces and control of his will-power" (Clausewitz, 1993, Book Four, p. 270). The enemy's will could be tested by different activities: prolonged resistance, waiting passively for the enemy assault, attrition, conquered territory, destruction of military force, occupation (see for example Clausewitz, 1993, Book One, Chapter Two: "Purpose and Means in War") and the "dominant consideration" (but not the sole one) of "direct annihilation" (Clausewitz, 1993, Book Four, p. 270). Will was the objective, as much as high ground or a key fortress. How was the enemy's will to be overthrown?

"Moral factors" and managed ccommunication

"[S]ubtleties of logic do not motivate the human will" (Clausewitz, 1993, Book One, p. 87). He also believed that the will could be understood and predicted (Clausewitz, 1993, Book One, p. 87). The keys to what motivate or undermine will are "moral factors". Sir Michael Howard reminds us that "Clausewitz was more concerned with analysing and explaining the differences" than the similarities between the wars of the French Revolution and the *ancien régime*" (Howard, 1976, "Clausewitz was yet"). Because of those differences, as we have seen, he believed war "was at least as much a matter of moral and political factors as of military expertise" (Howard, 1976, "War, he insisted").

Moral factors and political factors were inseparable, and the relationship between the two is of the utmost importance in understanding some of the directions taken by communication management. What Clausewitz describes as morals are the forces that reinforce or alter perception. Victory requires three things: greater material loss by the enemy, shrinking morale and "his open admission of the above by giving up his intentions" (Clausewitz, 1993, Book Four, p. 277). A vital contributor to success, for instance, is "shame and humiliation". "It is the only element that affects public opinion outside the army; that impresses the people and the governments of the two belligerents and of their allies" (Clausewitz, 1993, Book Four, p. 277). After the wars of the French Revolution and Napoleon, and powerful national identities that it aroused and needed, the stakes of defeat were raised from matters of dynastic succession and territorial adjustments of often indifferent peoples to—potentially—the fate of a great nation's government. Howard shows this in the diaries kept by German officers during the 1870–71 Franco-Prussian war: "the whole French nation must be made sick of fighting"; "no peace that does not dismember France, and the French Government"; "treat the French as a conquered army and demoralise them to the utmost of our ability" (Howard, 1961, p. 228). They more or less got their wishes, despite Bismarck's greater caution. The stakes had indeed been raised, with more extreme ideas about what conquest should mean, producing in the global totalitarian struggles of the twentieth century, intense local conflicts between modern states, and the Nuclear Age. These are dreadful answers to Clausewitz's questions in the eighth and final volume of *On War*:

> Will this always be the case in future? From now on will every war in Europe be waged with the full resources of the state, and therefore have to be fought only over major issues that affect the people? Or shall we again see a gradual separation between government and people?
> (Clausewitz, 1993, Book Eight, p. 717)

A further perspective on the role of communication appears when Clausewitz cautions the reader about unintended impacts on national will. A planned, orderly abandonment of the battlefield is for example hard to distinguish from either a defeat or a manoeuvre, and "the impression produced by the former, both in military and civilian circles, should not be underrated" (Clausewitz, 1993, Book Four, p. 277). He was aware that victory was a communication opportunity to be exploited, if necessary at the expense of accuracy: "Public accounts of the battle" produced by a victor "even if they are embellished by a few added details, will make it fairly evident to the rest of the world as well that the causes were general rather than particular" (Clausewitz, 1993, Book Four, p. 301). The communication care these situations require are described in Walter Lippmann's influential *Public Opinion* (1922), and his comments on the French Army's careful efforts to word a communiqué about a critical German assault at the siege of Verdun in the First World War:

> Within a few hours those two or three hundred words would be read all over the world. They would paint a picture in men's minds of what was

happening on the slopes of Verdun, and in front of that picture people would take heart or despair. The shopkeeper in Brest, the peasant in Lorraine, the deputy in the Palais Bourbon, the editor in Amsterdam or Minneapolis had to be kept in hope, and yet prepared to accept possible defeat without yielding to panic.

(Lippmann, 1997, p. 24)

Such dilemmas were one outcome of the Clausewitzian view that modern wars are fought between states, between the wills of governments and peoples as well as armies. If then moral factors were much more essential to war than in the past, so is the requirement to cultivate them in advance. Only "daring leadership" in war counteracts "the softness and the desire for ease which debase the people in times of growing prosperity and increasing trade" (Clausewitz, 1993, Book Three, p. 226). "A people and nation" Clausewitz wrote: "can hope for a strong position in the world only if national character and familiarity with war fortify each other by continual interaction" (Clausewitz, 1993, Book Three, p. 226).

This objective inevitably leads to the increasingly intensive management of words, images, and related media by the State before and during wars to create a "pseudo-environment" that captures an interpretation of the facts (Lippmann, 1997 edn, p. 24). The First World War German High Command established the UFA film company to produce war propaganda. The US Government established the Committee on Public Information, or Creel Committee, to prepare and maintain national will for participation in the war. Britain created a War Propaganda Bureau; the Italians a "P Service" after the disastrous defeat of Caporetto in 1917. Adolf Hitler drew many of his own views on propaganda from this conflict, particularly when the Allies suffered heavy defeats: "What propaganda and ingenious demagogy were used to hammer the faith in final victory back into the hearts of the broken fronts!" (Hitler, 1925, p. 188). Nevertheless, the German High Command had thoroughly managed national will in the First World War. When it finally called for an Armistice, because the army was "at the end of its tether": "It was a terrible shock to the politicians who had never been given the whole truth by the General Staff" (Lee, 2005, pp. 177–78).

Huw Strachan in *The First World War* is among those pointing out the continued management of the moral factor after the war, by finding a meaning for the struggle that resonated with public opinion: "When the British struck their Victory Medal for issue to all those who had served, they provided one answer: 'For Civilization'" (Strachan, 2005, "When the British struck"). Across the world, unknown soldiers were laid to rest, minutes of silence observed and cenotaphs and local memorials erected. "The biggest memorial in Germany, erected at Tannenberg in 1927, trumpeted a victory" (Strachan, 2005, "The biggest memorial"). In 1918 the new socialist Chancellor Francis Ebert had welcomed the German Army home saying "I salute you who return unvanquished from the field of battle" (Strachan, 2005, "I salute you"). The troops wore laurel wreaths over their helmets. New forces for unity had been unloosed, empires and states were crashing to the ground, and national will had to be protected as much as possible—it would be needed in future.

Total war, total PR

[M]ost of the matters dealt with in this book are composed in equal parts of physical and moral causes and effects. One might say that the physical seem little more than the wooden hilt, while the moral factors are the precious metal, the real weapon, the finely honed blade.

(Clausewitz, 1993, Book Three, p. 24)

Clausewitz's effect on communication with society helps explain his continuing relevance. Writing in 1955 about democracy's modern wars, Clausewitz translator Colonel Edward M. Collins (USAAF) gave communication-centred answers to Clausewitz's above-mentioned questions about war's future. As yet, Collins reported, there had been no separation of government from people in war. The former still needed the latter: "authoritarian governments have vastly greater power to influence and control their citizens; democratic governments possess a measure of this power" (Collins, 1955, p. 15).

On War's treatment of emotion and perception still has significance for the wars in the Middle East, in Afghanistan, or Vietnam. Clausewitz was concerned with breaking the morale of the enemy population: achieving a victory to overwhelm the will of the enemy's government and people—"a sudden collapse of the most anxious expectations and a complete crushing of self-confidence. ... This leaves a vacuum that is filled by a corrosively expanding fear, which completes the paralysis" (Clausewitz, 1993, Book Four, p. 303).

As we have also seen, he made general, impressionistic, recommendations for reinforcing popular will, describing the general need or posing related problems without offering communication solutions. For instance: engagements (not necessarily defeats) followed by retreats "can make a very bad impression. It is not possible for a general in retreat to forestall this moral effect by making his intentions known" (Clausewitz, 1993, Book Four, p. 278).

However, what he offered as general impressions and guiding principles were influential enough, because of *On War*'s enormous influence on military thinking. Clausewitz's emphasis on moral factors brings us to the rise of highly militarized states, to citizen armies supplied by mass manufacturing, carried into battle by mass transportation. The citizens are motivated by ideas about national manifest destiny, a place in the sun, *revanchism,* mass propaganda, and the doctrine of the major combatants that right down to the tactical level stressed willpower as *cran* (guts) or *élan.* From the First World War to the present, the business of warmaking must maintain the will to fight. The need to communicate determination and willpower is near-perpetual, another outcome of Clausewitz's legacy. It is apparent in large-scale propaganda, controlled and presented as news and entertainment, increasing intolerance of alternatives, volatile popular passion and careful management of sensitive issues (often known as Issues Management in modern PR):

> Having created in the public mind a belief that the aim of the war is to preserve the nation and/or its way of life, the political leaders set in motion currents which they are powerless to control. They cannot then represent the motive for the war in its true political light. Further, the emotional mood created in the people feeds back to the leaders and tends to make their attitude toward the war correspond to the image which they have themselves created.
>
> (Collins, 1955, p. 18)

After Clausewitz, it was seen that the close political management of communication was imperative, but this political dimension did not necessarily preserve a role for reason in warfare, as he hoped. The link between politics and war has strengthened since Clausewitz made his observations on the Napoleonic War's lessons. Under the pressures of time, space and attention created by communication technology the management of war-making emotion was distilled into simplifications—good versus evil, crusades against dangerous ideas, freedom versus tyranny. These were often crude, but thanks to vivid, authoritative or dramatic presentation techniques these messages are not without influence even today. The first exemplars of this new understanding were Moltke, and also Chancellor Otto von Bismarck famously priming the German people for war in 1870 by editing the Ems Telegram about a discussion between the Prussian King and French Ambassador, and releasing an inflammatory version to the world's press and to foreign governments, to goad the French and trigger the Franco-Prussian war he saw as inevitable, at a time of his own choosing. He succeeded. "Both in Berlin and in Paris excited crowds gathered shouting 'to the Rhine!'" (Howard, 1961, p. 55)

The result for communication was more management of feeling and spontaneity, by organizations with more communication resources. The result for war making was that managed communication held power over politicians and armies. Many democracies have developed to the point where, according to a penetrating sociological study of *On War*: "mass citizenship participation means that at some level at least political leaders must engage in public debate over war aims" (Roxborough, 1994, p. 629). It is also true that Clausewitz's simple categorization of "the people" was too crude for his own time and certainly for ours: "The 'people' likewise, must cease to be the homogenous mass depicted by Clausewitz, and be replaced in a neo-Clausewitzian sociology by an account that is nuanced in terms of class, organisation, gender, religion, region, age, race, etc." (Roxborough, 1994, p. 631).

This seems to be what has happened. The public communication activities of democratic governments are sensitive to nuance, and can engage "the people" as particular target audiences with messages about national unity or defence. They can connect with, isolate, create or invigorate audience identities according to need or belief. Clausewitz's impressionistic account of the moral factor has helped make societies (some democratic, some totalitarian) where views are more coordinated and managed than at any point in history. What started as a reaction to national emergencies continues much of the rest of the time, in a world of perpetual volatility. This legacy of *On War* is unlikely to have been expected by its author.

References

Clausewitz, C. (1993) *On War.* New York: Knopf.

Collins, E. M. (1955) "Clausewitz and Democracy's Modern Wars." *Military Affairs,* 19(1): 15–20.

Davis, D. E. and Kohn, W. S. (1977) "Lenin's Notebook on Clausewitz." *Soviet Armed Forces Review Annual,* 1: 188–229.

Hitler, A. (1971 [1925]). *Mein Kampf.* Translated by R. Mannheim. Boston, MA: Houghton Mifflin.

Howard, M. (1961) *The Franco-Prussian War: The German Invasion of France, 1870–1871.* New York: Macmillan.

——(1976) *War in European History.* London: Oxford University Press.

Lee, J. (2005) *The Warlords: Hindenburg and Ludendorff.* London: Weidenfeld & Nicolson.

Lippmann, W. (1997) *Public Opinion.* New York: Free Press Paperbacks.

Oki, T. (2011) "Clausewitz in 21st Century Japan". In R. Pommerin (ed.) *Clausewitz Goes Global: Carl von Clausewitz in the 21st Century. Commemorating the 50th Anniversary of the Clausewitz Society.* Berlin: Carola Hartmann Miles-Verlag, 203–8.

Roxborough, I. (1994) "Clausewitz and the Sociology of War." *The British Journal of Sociology,* 45(4): 619–36.

Strachan, H. (2005) *The First World War.* New York: Penguin.

7 PR, scientific inquiry and utopian mysticism

Karl Marx (1818–83) and Frederick Engels (1820–95), *The Communist Manifesto* (1848)

"Hybrid" PR

The Communist Manifesto was the agent of a worldwide revolution in managed public communication, and a considerable medium in its own right. Understanding its success on both counts involves exploring the *Manifesto's* hybrid style and content. It unites emotions unlocked by the Romantic era, industrial age economic and sociological study and analysis, and places them at the disposal of a cause. This union of data, passion and cause resulted in a form of public communication that continues to be exploited in the present day.

The Communist Manifesto inspired some of the most dynamic and imaginative PR materials ever centered on a single theme, and also some of the most leaden. For a short time the intensity of the effort surpassed Christianity and Islam. Organizations propagated the *Manifesto's* messages with books, pamphlets, slogans, film, music, fashion, newspapers and magazines, animation, posters, sport, the classroom, art, crockery, novels, world fairs, Russian nesting dolls, stage plays, architecture, ceremonies, decorated "agit trains" that brought much of the foregoing to rural communities. Human exemplars like Rosa Luxemburg, Lenin, Stalin or designs like the hammer and sickle, and "CCCP" are displayed today and venerated by many hopeful people in ways that symbols of other totalitarian creeds, almost equally murderous, are not. This should be no surprise. Communism pursued revolution, and innovation and exhilaration in communication is always invigorated by that heady prospect, as it had been in the Reformation and French Revolution. The nineteenth and twentieth centuries were intensely revolutionary. *The Communist Manifesto*, the 1848 revolutions, the 1871 Paris Commune, the 1917 October revolution in Russia, Mao's triumph in China and the independence struggles and insurgencies of the 1960s energetically celebrated and legitimized the victory Marx and Engels had predicted. Like Luther (and several comparisons with the *Ninety-five Theses* appear in this Chapter) a compelling style attracted the supporters of a large audience who "have nothing to lose but their chains" (Marx and Engels, 1998, p. 77). It was a call to rise, and quite in the spirit of other calls made in the Romantic era. "ARMINIUS!—all the people quaked like dew/Stirr'd by the breeze—they rose, a Nation, true," (Wordsworth, 1807). "Shades of the Helots! triumph o'er your foe:/ Greece! change thy lords, thy state is still the same;" (Byron, 1812, Canto II, v LXXVI).

In such heady atmospheres, the communication potential of almost every artefact is energized, ultimately expanding the possibilities of expression for PR beginning with propaganda. Marx was aware of this word, although it only appears once in the *Manifesto,* as a passing criticism.

In PR terms, the *Manifesto's* objective, language and the communication environment are on a different level to the works described so far. It sees its audiences in a new way, not through the usual fixed social structures accepted by moderate, literate, thinking, God-fearing observers. It creates two collective identities and arms one with powerful messages and media, to help them take power into their own hands, by pursuing a common goal via a series of steps that could be applied wherever conditions were right for revolution. This act of communication did not depend on passion alone. It also used scientific methods of inquiry and economic argument to radicalize the Industrial Revolution and the social conditions it made. The impact of this hybrid on managed public communication itself has also been global, very practical and at certain times highly effective.

One reason for that was that Marx and Engels wanted readers not only to think, but also to feel, and feel strongly. Despite its economic and sociological reasoning, and its criticism of utopian socialism, the *Manifesto* nonetheless foresees another utopia, but built on a scientifically argued foundation, with economic and social research attached to a powerful attack on social conditions resembling Part One of More's *Utopia* (1516). It also makes its case with a certainty reminiscent of Luther at his most outraged and of Clausewitz at his most definitive. *Manifesto* was written by two men in their late twenties for the newly formed (and short-lived) Communist League, "founded for purposes of education and propaganda" (Schumpeter, 1949, p. 199). It seeks to define, to outrage but most of all to overturn, to revolutionize and remake society. Its agents are the proletarians, those workers of the world who are urged so dramatically to unite at the end of the *Manifesto.*

The material justifications for this might be painstakingly researched—if narrowly based on Engels' study of the cotton industry and living conditions in South Lancashire in the UK—but stylistically *Manifesto* remains an offshoot of the Romantic era, and the turbulence stirred up by industrialism: "A spectre is haunting Europe—the spectre of Communism" it begins (Marx and Engels, 1998, p. 33). This is not a dry survey of social conditions, and nor is it pure invective, but a fusion of the two around a vivid objective.

The proletariat are summoned on stage in a similar stirring style. We have already seen that Lenin discussed Marx's interest in Clausewitz, and Marx and Engels appear to have adopted one of the two kinds of warfare described in *On War,* the one waged to "*overthrow the enemy*" and "render him politically helpless or militarily impotent" rather than a limited war for bargaining purposes (Clausewitz, 1993, p. 77). Lenin also suggests Marx agreed with the thesis that "war is nothing but the continuation of policy with other means" (Clausewitz, 1993, p. 77). In its content and style *The Communist Manifesto* adapts this into warfare by policy, if not necessarily by armed force. Military terms are deployed to explain the political opportunities the new industrial conditions had created:

> Masses of labourers, crowded into the factory, are organized like soldiers. As privates of the industrial army they are placed under the command of a perfect hierarchy of officers and sergeants. Not only are they slaves of the bourgeois class, and of the bourgeois state; they are daily and hourly enslaved by the machine.
>
> (Marx and Engels, 1998, p. 43)

The main traits of the *Manifesto* are well known. Perhaps its repercussions for PR are not, but they are inseparable from the rest. As well as spotting a political opportunity the authors numbered among those commentators alert to how drastically industrialization and urbanization changed the prospects for large-scale communication of opinion. It could now be done not only by the State; businesses and social movements could join in. In fact, as Eric Hobsbawm records, the book appeared at a moment when nationalism, radicalism, liberalism and urban unrest seemed to collide in a dramatic manifestation of the popular willpower identified by Clausewitz, and celebrated in their own ways by poets like Wordsworth, Byron or Heinrich Heine. "By good luck it [the *Manifesto*] hit the streets only a week or two before the outbreak of the revolutions of 1848, which spread like a forest fire from Paris across the continent of Europe" (Hobsbawm in Marx and Engels, 1998, p. 4).

The failure of 1848 and Marx's London exile in 1849 were temporary checks to the *Manifesto's* success, but new editions continued to appear and accelerated from about 1871, motivated by the rise and fall of the Paris Commune: "Over the next forty years the *Manifesto* conquered the world, carried forward by the rise of the new (socialist) labour parties, in which the Marxist influence rapidly increased in the 1880s" (Hobsbawm in Marx and Engels, 1998, p. 6).

The 1917 Russian Revolution ensured the book became "a political classic *tout court*" (Hobsbawm in Marx and Engels, 1998, p. 10), studied by earnest activists, scarcely less earnest academics, long-suffering schoolchildren, indoctrinated cadres, thoughtful workers seeking explanations for their plight and prospects, politicians in search of ideals, ideologies or supporters. It raised the incredible prospect of a world where unfairness, oppression and even politics could actually be abolished; it even changed the ways people talked to each other. Friends became *comrades*, workers were *proletariat*, classes were locked in *struggles*. It even explained the steps by which the change would happen—because it *was* going to happen: it was written into the laws of history. This belief that inevitability was scientifically, logically proved was one of the *Manifesto's* assets, even though the authors themselves had wrestled with that projection soon after publication in 1848, when it became clear that they had "reached overly pessimistic conclusions about the economic plight of the working class and overestimated the potential for a proletarian revolution" (Boyer, 1998, p. 169).

The "communication equity" of the *Manifesto* as an artefact arguably exceeds all the other works studied here, if we define it by the numbers and cultural diversity of the people it inspired, the attraction of the message it contained, its outcomes, and the extent of the damage it inflicted. Those outcomes have not been long-lasting, at least so far: but it is a condition of all great works that they experience continuous reinterpretation, involving analytical fine-tuning—sometimes ultra-fine tuning—and reinvention, and the *Manifesto* may show the same adaptive potential. Its message is still embedded in intellectual inquiry, it has influenced and even controlled many academic disciplines (offering scholars an opportunity to sound scientifically impenetrable, objective and subjective at the same time) and created scholars committed to keeping alive what they believe it represents.

Rationalism and irrationalism in the *Manifesto*

Marx and Engels gave a direction to existing discontents. The parallel with Luther appears again when we remind ourselves that, as with criticism of Church abuses, many of the *Manifesto's* distinguished contemporaries were also raging against the industrial machine, and searching for leaders to prize off its grip. The famous essayist Thomas Carlyle (1795–1881), for instance, was popular with left and right. In 1875 he complained that cash payment was "the sole nexus between man and man" in industrial capitalist society, and was supported by Engels (Engels, 1908, "Cash payment became"). Carlyle's 1840 lectures on The Hero, published in 1841 as *On Heroes, Hero-Worship and the Heroic in History*, lamented:

> [H]e who discerns nothing but Mechanism in the Universe has in the fatalest way missed the secret of the Universe altogether ... The "Doctrine of Motives" will teach him that it is, under more or less disguise, nothing but a wretched love of Pleasure, fear of Pain; that Hunger, of applause, of cash, of whatsoever victual it may be, is the ultimate fact of man's life.
>
> (Carlyle, 1908, p. 401)

Like Carlyle and other poets and essayists of this period, Marx and Engels accepted the reality of the Mechanism, and the "Doctrine of Motives". Unlike Carlyle they believed it presaged a society that would be more harmonious than Clausewitz with his views on the eternal clash of national wills; more egalitarian than Plato, Confucius and al-Farabi with their philosopher kings; more communal than Luther's advocacy of a personal relationship with

God. These ideas were supplanted by an organized, secular, rational, material, communal—communist—perspective on the human condition, somewhat reminiscent of the cooperative society of traders and farmers in More's *Utopia.* No trace of the Divine was visible. In the Preface to *A Contribution to the Critique of Political Economy* (1859) Marx reiterated the message of the *Manifesto.* The political, legal and economic relations between people are made by the "social production of their existence" or more specifically "relations of production" between people (Marx, 1977, "In the social production").

Yet Marx could not altogether ignore the lure of the irrational. He identified a far less rational, more spiritual, element in society's connection to capitalism: its fascination with commodities—in this case finished products. A commodity "is a very strange thing, abounding in metaphysical subtleties and theological niceties" (Marx, 1990, p.163). Marx dissected this relationship, seeking to demystify it by exposing its measurable and therefore (to him) more solid and potentially politicized characteristics. In Volume 1 of *Capital* (1867), he devoted a section to "The Fetishism of the Commodity and its Secret". "The mysterious character of the commodity form" may in reality arise from "the social characteristics of men's own labour as objective characteristics of the products of labour themselves" (Marx, 1990, pp. 164–65). Unfortunately the relationship that finished objects have between each other affects the relation between admiring eye and object and transcends the "quantitative determination of value" (Marx, 1990, p. 164) in favour of other values analogous to "the misty realm of religion". "I call this the fetishism which attaches itself to the products of labour as soon as they are produced as commodities, and is therefore inseparable from the production of commodities" (Marx, 1990, p. 165). For this reason a completed table, he amusingly explained:

[N]ot only stands with its feet on the ground, but, in relation to all other commodities, it stands on its head, and evolves out of its wooden brain grotesque ideas, far more wonderful than if it were to begin dancing of its own free will.

(Marx, 1990, p. 165)

Perhaps it is not a big step from this analysis to see that there would in time emerge mediators of this fetishist relationship between object and consumer, appointed by capitalists unwilling to leave it to chance, but there is nothing here from Marx about a priesthood of publicity, marketing and advertising. For him the fetishism of the commodity ceases when material production "becomes production by freely associated men, and stands under their consciousness and planned control", and that can only happen when popular perception is changed: "The religious reflections of the real world can, in any case, when the practical relations of every day life between man and man, and man and nature, generally present themselves to him in a transparent and rational form (Marx, 1990, p. 173).

What is instructive is to explore how Marx, Engels and their later followers invoked the powerful emotions behind "fetishism"—a misty religious quality— to give allure to the contents of their own finished product, *The Communist Manifesto.* We will now see how this developed.

Constructing a passionate identity

Marx and Engels ushered two audiences into political existence, gave them an identity, an economic life and a purpose that sustained Communism for a century and a half and remains a powerful political and economic agent. It is particularly interesting because of the fetishist qualities their analysis took on, because of the imaginative ways different media gave them life, and also because the audiences themselves are somewhat fluid and hard to pin down in real life. This problem required flexibility in managed public communication and in policy proposals, and healthy—and sometimes cruel and tragic—dissension between Communists. The differences lent vitality to communicating with their audiences, which finally fossilized in the last years of Communist government in Eastern Europe.

Marx had studied Roman law. From the Roman Census, especially those made in the Republican period, he identified the lowest social category of *proletarian.* It constituted people with offspring, but little or no property, earning a living from their labour for the property of others. They were the landless workers flooding into Rome until in the second century BC "the stringency of war conditions eventually broke down the proletarian mode of life with its cheap corn and games" (McDonald, 1939, p. 143).

This was the root of a far more sophisticated piece of audience analysis than previous distinctions between common people and kings, or rich and poor, even when these were converted into policy platforms, for instance by the future Tory Prime Minister Benjamin Disraeli. His account of "two nations"—"THE RICH AND THE POOR"—was a central element in his best-selling political and romantic novel *Sybil* (Disraeli, 1980, p. 95), which appeared in 1845, three years before *The Communist Manifesto.*

The crucial difference with Disraeli was that Marx and Engels' proletariat were not to think of themselves as poor, as dignified recipients of charity, or individuals seeking self-improvement, but as collectively proud and powerful, and the natural governors of a society eventually unconstrained by national boundaries, liberated from the "new conditions of oppression" (Marx and Engels, 1998, p. 35) that had grown out of more stratified pre-modern socie- ties. They are a class empowered by the great industrial and trading system they are destined to bring down.

The proletariat is immediately named in the first section of the *Manifesto,* as a distinct and vital identity worthy of close attention. It is an interesting contrast to the supporting roles popular audiences play in most of the works explored earlier. In *The Communist Manifesto,* they are the owners and ben- eficiaries of the main idea. The organizing principle for society (ostensibly) comes directly *from* them, not *to* them from heaven, or a more perfected person or group.

The proletariat fulfils the conditions of any target publics, including the one identified by Luther. To begin with, it has an entrenched adversary, as did Luther's restless god-fearing burgers. The *Manifesto* explains in the first section that "two great hostile camps", "two great classes, directly face each other: Bourgeois and Proletariat" (Marx and Engels, 1998, p. 35). The bourgeois are "the product of a long course of development, of a series of revolutions in the mode of production and of exchange" (Marx and Engels, 1998, p. 36). As they developed and exploited changes in communication, manufacturing and trade they subverted older orders of government and identity and substituted "no other nexus between man and man than naked self-interest, than callous cash payment" (Marx and Engels, 1998, p. 37). Family relations became money relations; the professions as well as the workers became "its paid wage labourers" (Marx and Engels, 1998, pp. 37–38). "The executive of the modern state is but a committee for managing the common affairs of the whole bourgeoisie" (Marx and Engels, 1998, p. 37), who have also "subjected the country to the rule of the towns" (Marx and Engels, 1998, p. 40), "created enormous cities ... and [have] thus rescued a considerable part of the population from the idiocy of rural life" (Marx and Engels, 1998, p. 40). And as with the country, so globally the bourgeois "has made barbarian and semi-barbarian countries dependent on the civilized ones" (Marx and Engels, 1998, p. 40).

Marx and Engels famously describe the impact of this restless, creatively destructive group with an apocalyptic style Luther would have recognized, and perhaps also we who witness modern technological ferment:

> All fixed, fast-frozen relations, with their train of ancient and venerable prejudices and opinions, are swept away, all new-formed ones become antiquated before they can ossify. All that is solid melts into air, all that is holy is profaned and man is at last compelled to face with sober senses, his real conditions of life, and his relations with his kind.
>
> (Marx and Engels, 1998, pp. 38–39)

Under its wing, culture "is, for the enormous majority, a mere training to act as a machine" (Marx and Engels, 1998, p. 55); the bourgeois family "finds its complement in the practical absence of the family among the proletarians, and in public prostitution" (Marx and Engels, 1998, p. 56); women are "mere instruments of production" (Marx and Engels, 1998, p. 57); bourgeois marriage "is in reality a system of wives in common" (Marx and Engels, 1998, p. 57).

The violent economic fluctuations ("commercial crises") that Marx and Engels saw around them seemed proof that the bourgeois "is like the sorcerer, who is no longer able to control the powers of the nether world whom he has called up by his spells" (Marx and Engels, 1998, p. 41), and each crisis threatened the future of bourgeois society: "The weapons with which the bourgeoisie felled feudalism to the ground are now turned against the bourgeoisie itself" (Marx and Engels, 1998, p. 42). In other, yet more damning words: "its existence is no longer compatible with society ... What the bourgeoisie, therefore, produces, above all, is its own grave-diggers. Its fall and the victory of the proletariat are equally inevitable" (Marx and Engels, 1998, p. 50).

Activating the audience

Creating two sides, and "targeting" one as an opponent, introduces another military dimension to the *Manifesto's* communication. A point will come when the veiled civil war between the classes "breaks out into open revolution, and where the violent overthrow of the bourgeoisie lays the foundation for the sway of the proletariat " (Marx and Engels, 1998, p. 49). "Overthrow of the bourgeois supremacy" cannot be achieved without the "formation of the proletariat into a class"; a class moreover that is organized, disciplined and unified (Marx and Engels, 1998, p. 51).

The bourgeois brought the proletariat into an active existence as "a really revolutionary class" ready to oust the oppressor. The proletariat is composed of labourers, and the "lower strata of the middle class—the small tradespeople, shopkeepers, retired tradesmen generally, the handicraftsmen and peasants" (Marx and Engels, 1998, p. 44), and others continuously driven into its ranks by production changes. The capital of this group is too small to compete with modern bourgeois, especially after the disappearance of the Medieval Guilds that protected many of them. This "incoherent mass" (Marx and Engels, 1998, p. 45), hitherto scattered and unorganized, but now more urbanized, and very big, would come into its political inheritance.

Marx and Engel's next task, after identifying the proletariat and shaping a personality for its common opponent, was to make the proletariat accept its identity and its power, because: "with the development of industry the proletariat not only increases in number; it becomes concentrated in greater masses, its strength grows, and it feels that strength more" (Marx and Engels, 1998, p. 45).

With the audience identified, and its "opposing" audience, it remained for the authors to outline the steps by which the first would overcome the second: "The proletariat, the lowest stratum of our present society, cannot stir, cannot raise itself up, without the whole superincumbent strata of official society being sprung into the air" (Marx and Engels, 1998, p. 49). Bringing about such an event, they argued, must necessarily involve the helpfully ambiguous verb and noun "struggle", the less ambiguous "revolution", and occasionally the entirely unambiguous words "war" and possibly the above-mentioned need to be "violent", and above all to "fight".

To "fight", "struggle", "overthrow", was needed because "Communists everywhere support every revolutionary movement against the existing social and political order of things" (Marx and Engels, 1998, p. 77). Communists "declare that their ends can be attained only by the forcible overthrow of all existing conditions" (Marx and Engels, 1998, p. 77), the "conquest of political power" (Marx and Engels, 1998, p. 51).

Dreaming the objective

A plan this ambitious cannot succeed without a considerable communication effort to ensure the new audience is utterly committed to the identity fashioned for it, and to the logic that flows from belonging. Alternative and distracting nostrums of others on the left were extensively criticized in Section Three of the *Manifesto* as "reactionary socialism" made up of "Feudal Socialism", "Petty-Bourgeois Socialism" ("a miserable fit of the blues"), "German, or 'True' Socialism" ("foul and enervating"); "Conservative, or Bourgeois Socialism" and "Critical Utopian Socialism" ("compelled to appeal to the feelings and purses of the bourgeois").

Discipline and persuasion were critical to concentrate the will and common agreement for the Manifesto's radical methods and radical objectives, which "cannot be effected except by means of despotic inroads on the rights of property, and on the conditions of bourgeois production" (Marx and Engels, 1998, p. 60). Marx and Engels offered a program that was collective and severely secular: the abolition of property, heavy progressive income tax, the abolition of inheritance tax, "confiscation of the property of all emigrants and rebels" (Marx and Engels, 1998, p. 61), State control of credit by a national bank, State centralization of communication and transport, State ownership of factories and waste land, making all liable for labour and the: "Establishment of industrial armies, especially for agriculture", a "more equable" distribution of population (presumably forced), free education and abolition of child labour (Marx and Engels, 1998, p. 61).

What kind of society would this create? One in which "class distinctions have disappeared" into an "association of the whole nation" (Marx and Engels, 1998, p. 61). Marx and Engels evidently felt global change must be accomplished nation by nation, as the conditions for revolution existed in some nations—like Germany—more than others. Nevertheless, national struggles in different countries "bring to the front the common interests of the entire proletariat, independently of all nationality" (Marx and Engels, 1998, p. 51).

Managed public communication is where the utopian nature of the *Manifesto* elides yet more closely with the commonwealth envisaged by Sir Thomas More. In his *Utopia* criticism of the system is no longer necessary. Under the new collective conditions of Communism, "the public power will lose its political character": "Political power, properly so called, is merely the organized power of one class for oppressing another" (Marx and Engels, 1998, p. 61).

After the revolution classes can no longer exist. The bourgeoisie have been destroyed, and the proletariat is no longer "compelled, by the force of circumstances, to organize itself as a class" (Marx and Engels, 1998, p. 61). Sweeping away class antagonism by doing away with the opposition also brings to an end the conditions for "classes generally" and the proletariat, having done its work "will thereby have abolished its own supremacy as a class" in favour of "an association, in which the free development of each is the condition for the free development of all" (Marx and Engels, 1998, p. 62). Engel's 1878 book *Socialism: Utopian and Scientific* (extracted from a larger polemic written in 1875) is no more detailed, despite having almost thirty more years to reflect on it; saying vaguely that seizing the means of production "gives their socialized character complete freedom to work itself out", suggesting that the final character of this process could not yet be guessed at (Engels, 1908, "By this act").

The detail of the future Communist State receives scarcely any attention in the *Manifesto*, which is concerned with how to get there, and with romantic visions of the promise it holds. Thirty years on *Socialism: Utopian and Scientific* only offered more of the same: "Man, at last the master of his own form of social organization, becomes at the same time the lord over Nature, his own master—free" (Engels, 1908, "Man, at last"). It is however obvious, crucially, that a massive concentration of power must rest in State hands as the people's representative; power more concentrated because there are more resources to be controlled than in the states imagined by al-Farabi, Plato and Confucius. This control is tightened by the communication, manufacturing and transportation power the State will have at its disposal. Nor is it clear how the many will be represented in a government that must inevitably be managed by a few representatives: who would they be? How would they wield a power that is meant to have lost its "political character"? Most relevant for us, what will there be to communicate in a political vacuum? Will Communism create a State of small communities and local communication, as in More's book? Or was it a State in which the tenets of Communism are constantly restated at every stage of life and passed down from the leaders, a secular version of al-Farabi? One of the *Manifesto*'s greatest oversights is not to explain the communication needed in a State where social differences, private property and politics have been abolished. Presumably, its authors felt the mass management of communication would disappear also, because a cooperative consensus would emerge that made it unnecessary. Few thinkers discussed here made the same mistake.

The omission nonetheless contributed to the peculiarity of revolutionary communication: tireless energy in inspiring, educating and showing target audiences what they must do to bring about Communism; yet growing lack of imagination, stale repetition and disengagement from the aspirations of target audiences once it had been safely established. It was inspiring communication to attack a system, but it lost its message once the old system was replaced. Nevertheless, communication had to continue because Communism has not, as it turned out, led to the abolition of politics. A political party came to power in Communist States, without at any point feeling ready to relinquish its privileges or abolish itself. To remain in power it resorted to Platonic and Confucian techniques: deciding which literature and poetry was unsuitable, managing art, the language of rites, and devising new ceremonials. The names of settlements and landscapes were changed. The calendar's steady energy was harnessed by creating new ritual moments in the year to substitute for the old. Music was as important to the first Communist States as it was to Plato. Lenin, Stalin, Mao (and others) "early commenced control of 'negative' music and of those who taught and performed it" (Perris, 1983, p. 2). Unsurprisingly, propaganda became one of the most powerful arms of government since it influenced the activities of other arms. After the Communist triumph in China, for instance, the State Propaganda Department in the 1950s controlled "the nation's cultural and literary activities, as well as setting their agendas" (Hung, 2005, p. 923).

In the USSR and in several other Communist States the founders were remembered as philosopher-kings, ultimately to be embalmed and/or enshrined to continue their work: Lenin in Red Square, Mao in Tiananmen Square, Bulgaria's Georgi Dimitrov in 9 September Square, North Korea's Kim Il-Sung in the Palace of the Sun.

The energy and attraction in Communism's managed public communication lies in the period of "struggle" described by the *Manifesto*. Marx was aware of the term "propaganda" as a motivational activity conducted by both sides, whilst assuming the Communist version operated on a higher level, by virtue of its perfection. In *Capital* Volume 1 he criticizes the ruinous impact of "Free-trade propaganda in the English interest" in Turkey (Marx, 1990, p. 912), and applies it pejoratively to a rival socialist activist for borrowing Marx's ideas without general acknowledgement (Marx, 1990, p. 89–90). Alternatively, in an earlier essay, he was insightful about the wider potential of propaganda, as something that could be both directly and indirectly applied:

> When communist workmen gather together, their immediate aim is instruction, propaganda, etc. But at the same time they acquire a new need—the need for society—and what appears as a means has become an end. This practical development can be most strikingly observed in the gatherings of French socialist workers. Smoking, eating and drinking, etc., are no longer means of creating links between people. Company, association, conversation, which in its turn has society as its goal, is enough for them.
>
> (Marx, 1992, Economic and Political Manuscripts)

Communicating struggle, and its limitations

The *Manifesto*'s internal structure and style, and its radical vision, led to a closer management of a coordinated message by central organizations with an incredible array of media. Everyday material things like a hammer, sickle or sheaf of wheat could be turned into communication artefacts, which Gandhi was also to realize. It was communication driven by strength of popular belief, a unified theme, and passions many (there were exceptions) businesses and traditional governments could not evoke, lacking the advantage of neb-ulous utopian promises. It became in every sense and form of media "art at the command of doctrine" (Perris, 1983, p. 1). Bernays marked the *Manifes-to's* impact on public opinion. In 1952 he advised: "in order to combat com-munism, the public relations techniques of the Communist party should receive the careful study of all those interested in preserving democracy" (Bernays, 1980, "At the outbreak of").

The tone and techniques used in the *Manifesto* cut deeper still. Its messages fired the Romantic idea that struggle was an end in itself. Struggle thrilled the soul, epitomized what it meant to be alive, and pumped unflagging energy into a noble purpose. It was communication for certainty, one single cause, organizing new media and messages behind a principle. These legacies are prized by popular single-issue campaigns today, and even some corporations offer creative variations on certainties of commercial faith. But what is there to do or say once the Cause is victorious, established and institutionalized? Silence on this question is the Manifesto's greatest communication failure.

References

Bernays, E. L. (1980) *Public Relations.* Norman: University of Oklahoma Press.

Boyer, G. R. (1998) "The Historical Background of The Communist Manifesto." *The Journal of Economic Perspectives*, 12(4): 151–74.

Byron, Lord G. (2012 [1812]) "Childe Harold's Pilgrimage" In *Delphi Complete Works of Lord Byron.* Delphi Classics.

Carlyle, T. (1908) "*Sartor Resartus,* and *On Heroes, Hero-worship and the Heroic in History.*" London: J. M. Dent & Sons. Retrieved from www.gutenberg.org/ebooks/20585.

Clausewitz, C. (1993) *On War.* New York: Knopf.

Disraeli, B. (1980) *Sybil: Or, the Two Nations.* Edited by T. Braun with and Intro-duction by R. A. Butler. Harmondsworth: Penguin Books.

Engels, F. (1908) *Socialism: Utopian and Scientific.* Public Domain.

Hung, C. T. (2005) "The Red Line: Creating a Museum of the Chinese Revolution." *The China Quarterly London*, 184 (Dec.): 914–33.

Marx, K. (1977) "Preface *A Contribution to the Critique of Political Economy.*" Moscow: Progress Publishers. Retrieved from www.marxists.org/archive/marx/works/1859/critique-pol-economy/preface.htm.

——(1992) *Early Writings.* Harmondsworth: Penguin in association with *New Left Review.*

Marx, K. (1990) *Capital: A Critique of Political Economy.* Translated by B. Fowkes. London: Penguin Books in association with *New Left Review.*

Marx, K. and Engels, F. (1998) *The Communist Manifesto: A Modern Edition.* With an introduction by E. J. Hobsbawm. London: Verso.

McDonald, A. H. (1939) "The History of Rome and Italy in the Second Century BC" *Cambridge Historical Journal*, 6(2): 124–46.

Perris, A. (1983) "Music as Propaganda: Art at the Command of Doctrine in the People's Republic of China." *Ethnomusicology*, 27(1): 1–28.

Schumpeter, J. A. (1949) "The Communist Manifesto in Sociology and Economics." *The Journal of Political Economy*, 57(3), 199–212.

Wordsworth, W. (2013 [1807]). "High deeds, O Germans, are to come from you!" In *Delphi Complete Works of William Wordsworth*. Delphi Classics.

8　Proofing against puffing
John Stuart Mill (1806–73),
On Liberty (1859)

Publicity for the majority, by the majority

On Liberty, like the *Ninety-five Theses* and *The Communist Manifesto*, has shaped ideas about freedom. Admirers are found across the political spectrum. Britain's Liberal Democrat Party claims the author himself. In 2009 the Liberal Democrat History Group voted Mill the greatest British Liberal in history after a debate (Liberal Democrat History Group, 2009). Every incoming President of the Party is presented with a copy of *On Liberty*. Elsewhere the classical liberal Friedrich von Hayek praised Mill's "great essay" (Hayek, 2007, "It overlooks the") in *The Road to Serfdom* (1944), though he would have little sympathy with the Lib Dems, especially as he resented the left's appropriation of the term "Liberal", moving it from classical liberalism toward statism, deliberately confusing meaning to win political advantage. Gertrude Himmelfarb, historian of Victorian Britain, and a more traditional conservative, wrote on the "Other Mill": "He has shown us that a Liberal cannot be wholly a Liberal, but must often be a better Tory than Tories themselves" (Himmelfarb, 2006, p. 120). Mill himself, a believer in both economic and social liberalism, spent three terms in parliament committed to the "defence of advanced Liberalism" (Mill, 1981, "The same idea"). He also described himself at one time in his life as a "socialist", during a period long pre-dating the British version's official commitment to nationalizing the means of production (Mill, 1981, "I then reckoned chimerical").

What attracts his diverse admirers? The editor of Chicago University's 2007 edition of *The Road to Serfdom* says *On Liberty* "defended the freedom of the individual in the face of political and social control" (Caldwell in Hayek, 2007, "In his book"). This view is correct, supported by many of Mill's views about freedom of speech, which also meant freedom from censorship. The freedoms Mill cherished sprang from the ruins of old managed public communication, which had appeared in the oldest works studied here:

> The ancient commonwealths thought themselves entitled to practice, and the ancient philosophers countenanced, the regulation of every part of private conduct by public authority, on the ground that the State had a

deep interest in the whole bodily and mental discipline of every one of its citizens.

(Mill, 1977b, "The ancient commonwealths")

What makes *On Liberty* different, not just from Confucius, Plato or al-Farabi, but from Marx, Engels and Clausewitz? Marx and Engels had identified the proletariat as the product of modern industrial conditions. In Mill's essays, articles and his later book *Utilitarianism*, the main point was that those conditions permitted "the formation and propagation of a public opinion" (Mill, 1985, "In the ancient"). "In politics it is almost a triviality to say that public opinion now rules the world" he declared (Mill, 1977b, "In sober truth"); commenting on "the complete establishment, in this and other free countries, of the ascendancy of public opinion in the State" (Mill, 1977b, "A more powerful"). For that reason—on the face of it a triumph for liberty—Mill feared public opinion was being standardized, by being communicated through mass media and uncritically received, producing a nation where "there ceases to be any social support for non-conformity" (Mill, 1977b, "A more powerful").

It is the first work after Luther studied here to connect individual freedom to public communication. It declared that public communication itself *is* freedom, or at least intimately connected with it, and must be available to all. Mill famously tried to balance the needs for freedom of expression with the rights of minorities, and head off a looming threat to liberty in an age of growing democracy and a popular press: "The disposition of mankind, whether as rulers or as fellow-citizens, to impose their own opinions and inclinations as a rule of conduct on others" (Mill, 1977b, "The disposition of ").

The right to free speech is "constitutive of Mill's free society—an ideal founded on his conception of the pre-requisites for human flourishing" (Jacobson, 2000, pp. 277–78). This is refreshing stuff, compared with the controls over perception management that most of our earlier works implicitly or explicitly advocated. *On Liberty* makes its case in a measured tightly written style that has little in common with the expansive romantic assertions in *The Communist Manifesto*, or even parts of *On War*. In this his father James influenced John. The elder Mill was a Scottish philosopher, utilitarian, historian and founder of classical economics with Adam Smith and David Ricardo, among others. In Bertrand Russell's lively words, James: "was utterly opposed to every form of romanticism. He thought politics could be governed by reason, and expected men's opinions to be determined by the weight of evidence" (Russell, 1961, p. 743). Marx was more interested in James than in John, and suspicious of the latter. *Capital* (Volume One, 1867) credited the son (among others) for aspiring "to be something more than mere sophists and sycophants of the ruling classes" which nevertheless produced no more than "a shallow syncretism", "a declaration of bankruptcy by the bourgeois economy" (Marx, 1990, p. 98).

On Liberty appeared shortly after the death of J. S. Mill's wife and intellectual partner Harriet, and some years after an intellectual crisis that turned him away from utilitarianism's drier nostrums. It is celebrated for the introductory chapter advocating absolute liberties for an age of industrialism, urbanism, and mass communication: "liberty of thought and feeling", "liberty of tastes and pursuits", liberty to combine and unite "for any purpose not involving harm to others" (Mill, 1977b, "But there is a sphere"). These definitions, combining public actions with emotional satisfactions, opened the door to a fresh perspective on public communication and its management:

> The liberty of expressing and publishing opinions may seem to fall under a different principle, since it belongs to that part of the conduct of an individual which concerns other people; but, being almost of as much importance as the liberty of thought itself, and resting in great part on the same reasons, is practically inseparable from it.
>
> (Mill, 1977b, "The liberty of expressing")

The citizen as communicator

It is evident that we are still largely in the realm of communication's relationship to government. It sometimes seems great thinkers cannot see the management of communication in any other way, until we reach Gandhi and von Hayek. As a classical economist and as philosopher, however, Mill cannot entirely divide his thought from the voluntary and business sectors and their own relationship with communication. We begin to trace the growing skill shown by non-government organizations at managing the new version of communication in the public arena. It was a product and a cause of that dynamism observed by Marx and Engels, which was breaking up the rigid audiences identified by pre-modern thinkers. Mill declared that: "as soon as mankind have attained the capacity of being guided to their own improvement by conviction or persuasion (a period long since reached in all nations with whom we need here concern ourselves)" compulsion and regulation as practiced in ancient and later States "is no longer admissible as a means to their own good, and justifiable only for the security of others" (Mill, 1977b, "Until then, there"). The communication conditions have changed. Humanity has "become capable of being improved by free and equal discussion" (Mill, 1977b, "Liberty, as a principle"). This secular and energetic public opinion undermined the approaches of antiquity, but did not necessarily lock people into the modern industrial audiences Marx and Engels tried to define. A closer parallel to Mill's thinking on this was the religious dissolution Luther activated. Another is French sociologist Gustave Le Bon (1841–1931), in his famous analysis *The Crowd: A Study of the Popular Mind* (1895). Le Bon acknowledged a "frivolous bourgeoisie" at the summit, and an "army of proletarians" at the bottom, but at the same time:

The working man no longer wishes to remain a working man, or the peasant to continue a peasant, while the most humble members of the middle classes admit of no possible career for their sons except that of State-paid functionaries.

(Le Bon, 2001, p. 54)

"From the top to the bottom of the social pyramid, from the humblest clerk to the professor and the prefect, the immense mass of persons boasting diplomas besiege the professions" (Le Bon, 2001, p. 54). It is a stampede toward personal, not collective, aspirations, creating audiences of a different cast of mind to proletariat and bourgeois, audiences of consumers, commuters, parents, national subjects and so on. As Romanticism merged with the consumer age, material and spiritual aspirations were ultimately pursued by individuals, "by myself". Carl Jung and von Hayek are responsive to this form of modernism, which John Updike defined as "a self-consciousness new among centuries, a consciousness of being new" (Kafka, 1983, Foreword). Mill also recognized it: "Over himself, over his own body and mind, the individual is sovereign" (Mill, 1977b, "Over himself").

For the sovereign individual, Mill cited America, a society with minimal government intervention: "let them be left without a government, every body of Americans is able to improvise one" he optimistically declared, aware of the country's internal divisions, while more hopeful for America's prospects than continental Europe's. "No bureaucracy can hope to make such a people as this do or undergo anything that they do not like" (Mill, 1977b, "A very different spectacle).

The citizen as target audience

It is now we see the contradictions that Mill wrestles with, and the problems for managing public communication. At first Mill seems blunt: "All attempts by the State to bias the conclusions of its citizens on disputed subjects, are evil" (Mill, 1977b, "All attempts by"); or: "The time, it is to be hoped, is gone by when any defence would be necessary of the 'liberty of the press'" (Mill, 1977b, "The time, it is"); and again: "I deny the right of the people to exercise such coercion, either by themselves or their government" (Mill, 1977b, "But I deny"). Has a leading thinker at last located that long-sought society in which managed, or controlled, communication is unnecessary, this time because a fully realized citizen can manage it for him or herself? Unlike Marx and Engels, Mill does not shirk the details of such a society in the fifth and final Chapter of *On Liberty*, "Applications". Some of these details concerned him, particularly the possibility that a true democracy, with universal suffrage, could invest absolute power in a single large class, "alike in biases, prepossessions, and general modes of thinking, and a class, to say no more, not the most highly cultivated" (Mill, 1977c, "But even in this").

This comment was made in his 1861 essay "Considerations on Repre-sentative Government", and raises something the scholar of intellectual his-tory Joseph Hamburger discussed in his last work, *John Stuart Mill on Liberty and Control* (1999), "that Mill was just as concerned to implement various mechanisms of social control as he was to guard and protect indivi-dual liberties" (quoted in Wiland, 2001, p. 637). Hamburger concluded Mill's liberalism "was diminished by another, not obviously compatible belief in the need to subdue and control the inherent selfishness of human nature by imposing order and authority on it" (Hamburger, 1999, "From his more"). Is there any evidence of this, seen from the perspective of managing or even controlling public perception; and what is it saying about the evolution of public relations?

Mill characterized the potentially tyrannous majority as a single large, and not too well educated group, whose members are far less ennobled by the blessings of liberty than his earlier comments might imply. In his 1873 *Autobiography* he wrote of "the uncultivated herd who now compose the labouring masses" and the shortcomings of their employers, that prevented social transformation (Mill, 1981, "We saw clearly"). He was also con-cerned with the rise of the crowd phenomenon, and its new power in the industrial age, cultivated by the popular press, and its affect on the indi-vidual. These subjects preoccupied nineteenth-century commentators, filling them with dread or hope. The reaction of Marx and Engels has been recorded. Others were thinking about this kind of crowd. They included Carlyle, Le Bon, the philosopher Søren Kierkegaard, the novelist Edgar Allan Poe and even on occasion Sir Arthur Conan Doyle, author of Sherlock Holmes. A short piece by Kierkegaard (1813–55) "The Crowd is Untruth" (1847) was originally a dedication for another essay, but expanded into a short work:

> A crowd—not this or that, one now living or long dead, a crowd of the lowly or of nobles, of rich and poor, etc., but in its very concept—is untruth, since a crowd either renders the single individual wholly unre-pentant and irresponsible, or weakens his responsibility by making it a fraction of his decision.
>
> (Kierkegaard, 2009, "A crowd—not this")

Henceforth, thinkers in this book must resolve the communication relation-ship between individual and collective. In "Civilization" (1836), one of his earlier essays, Mill discussed a "little attended to" (Mill, 1977a, "But here presents") ramification of increased civilization brought about by population and urban growth, the crowd's power over public opinion, whenever an idea was successfully implanted in its collective head:

> There has been much complaint of late years, of the growth, both in the world of trade and in that of intellect, of quackery, and especially of

puffing; but nobody seems to have remarked that these are the inevitable fruits of immense competition.

(Mill, 1977a, "There has been")

"Puffing", a term for inflated and distorted publicity, creates "a state of society where any voice, not pitched in an exaggerated key, is lost in the hubbub" (Mill, 1977a, "There has been"). "The individual becomes so lost in the crowd, that though he depends more and more upon opinion, he is apt to defend less and less upon well-grounded opinion" (Mill, 1977a, "But here presents").

In business and civic affairs: "For the first time, arts for attracting public attention form a necessary part of the qualifications even of the deserving: and skill in these goes farther than any other quality towards ensuring success" (Mill, 1977a, "But here presents").

Mill inserted a long passage from an article written in 1832 (Mill, 1984), in which he declared that the power of the mass "corrupts the very fountain of the improvement of public opinion itself". Literature and mass literacy produced fewer good books that were read carefully or often "so much of the business is now transacted through the press, that it is necessary to know what is being printed, if we desire to know what is going on" (Mill, 1977a, "This is a reading age").

The themes are familiar to us, and maybe no less true for all their exaggeration: "what wonder that the newspapers carry all before them?" "Nothing is now read slowly, or twice over"; "not he who speaks more wisely, but he who speaks most frequently, obtains the influence" (Mill, 1977a, "This is a reading age") "The evils are, that the individual is lost and becomes impotent in the crowd, and that the individual character itself becomes relaxed and enervated" (Mill, 1977a, "The evils are"). The remedy? "[G]reater and more perfect combination among individuals" and "national institutions, forms of polity, calculated to invigorate the individual character" (Mill, 1977a, "The evils are").

Himmelfarb rightly says that "Civilization" foreshadows *On Liberty* (Himmelfarb, 2006, p. 105). The remainder of the essay proposes reforms of the universities to meet the new conditions. Wider reflection on the problem and remedy is the purpose of *On Liberty*. There must be a new approach to public opinion and it must be communicated, especially as Mill was deeply concerned with the role of literature in public life, and the public's ability to distinguish the good from the bad. In *On Liberty*, written over twenty years after "Civilization", Mill reiterates that this liberated, more literate, democratized new audience cannot be trusted to reform itself: "few think it necessary to take any precautions against their own fallibility". Absolute rulers have confidence in their opinions because they are rarely contradicted; the rest of us are confident "only on such of their opinions as are shared by all who surround them, or to whom they habitually defer" (Mill, 1977b, "Unfortunately for the good"). Today these may include the peer endorsers, activist groups and third party experts now essential to reputation and issues management campaigns, and to many corporate branding or social responsibility activities.

There is a fascinating moment of curiosity, too, when Mill asks himself how "the remarkable phenomenon of Mormonism" could be believed "by hundreds of thousands, and has been made the foundation of a society, in the age of newspapers, railways, and the electric telegraph" (Mill, 1977b, "Much might be said"). Here Mill seems to hope that increased velocity and volumes of information would increase wisdom and reason—a hope often expressed when new communication media appears, be it a printing press, a railway, television or the Internet. He also suspects his hope may not be realized. None of this nullifies the Mormon Church's right to exist, however strange it seems. When the majority feels infallible, as Mill saw it did in opposition to Mormonism, their press will use "the language of downright persecution", with "little account commonly made of human liberty" (Mill, 1977b, "I cannot refrain"). As the individual grows freer, like-minded masses of individuals grow more powerful, and the phrase used twenty three years earlier in "Civilization" is repeated in *On Liberty*: "At present individuals are lost in the crowd" (Mill, 1977b, "In sober truth"). Mill wanted that crowd to understand the conditions necessary for their freedom. Until that happened, he feared government coercion would follow the "yoke of opinion" once the majority learn "to feel the power of the government their power, or its opinions their opinions" (Mill, 1977b, "In England, from"). Marx and Engels had recognized and welcomed the mass as the proletariat; Mill viewed it as any majority intolerantly convinced its opinion represented the truth. For the present, *On Liberty* feared the power of that mass: "I deny the right of the people to exercise such coercion, either by themselves or by their government" (Mill, 1977b, "Let us suppose, therefore").

Hamburger says of this that "the inclusion of the constraint theme indicates that the title promises more than the author was prepared to allow" (Hamburger, 1999, "The title (and much … ").

Fitting publicity for States with liberty

In *On Liberty* public opinion is the arena where freedom is tested. Yet it is unclear what Mill thought public opinion was, or how it worked. These matters were not as important to him as what it was doing: destroying individuality, making people conform. The parallel he drew for public opinion was with the stagnation created by stifling any individuality in nineteenth-century China: "and unless individuality shall be successfully able to assert itself against this yoke" Europe "will tend to become another China" (Mill, 1977b, "We have a warning") with: "[T]he public, with the most perfect indifference, passing over the pleasure or convenience of those whose conduct they censure, and considering only their own preference" (Mill, 1977b, "But the strongest").

Mill therefore worried over what he described in one article as "the grand achievement of the present age which was the diffusion of superficial knowledge" (Mill, 1986a, "I am unable to"). He worried in *On Liberty* about people whose "thinking is done for them by men such as themselves, addressing them or speaking in their name, on the spur of the moment, through the newspapers" (Mill, 1977b, "In sober truth"). He worried that:

> Those whose opinions go by the name of public opinion, are not always the same sort of public" ... [I]n America, they are the whole white population; in England, chiefly the middle class. But they are always a mess, that is to say, collective mediocrity.
>
> (Mill, 1977b, "In sober truth")

"[T]he mass is productive of mischief" (Mill, 1977a, "This is a reading age"), but how could public opinion be honestly shaped? Mill endorsed "publicity", as opposed to "puffing". Proper publicity—"the light of publicity" (Mill, 1981, "Saturated as the book"; Mill, 1977c, "Instead of the functions") was essential to liberty, by allowing abuses or opinions to be presented to the public by informed persons. Mill's writings distinguished between "puffing" and "publicity". He wrote extensively for the newspapers himself, in which he often—as has been attempted here—described publicity's ancient lineage, for instance praising the "unbounded publicity" of Athenian political life, and its virtue as "a government of unlimited publicity". In contemporary affairs he valued the part publicity played in exposing abuses of the law, cruelty to women and children, and other marginal members of society, being for instance pleased that the "publicity of the inquiry" offers some protection to lunatics facing the possibility of incarceration by "foolish and credulous" juries (Mill, 1986b, letters 380, 391, 395, 396, 407).

Mill used publicity to try and reform public opinion, and more thoroughly than the works already examined.

What are his proposals? These are mainly (but not only) found in Chapter Five of *On Liberty*, "Applications", which seems something of a disappointment, like an unconsidered reaction to *On War*'s impressionistic discursions on willpower and the moral factor, or to the vague promises of *The Communist Manifesto*. Hamburger observes "where we might expect details, he [Mill] tells us there will only be enough detail 'to illuminate the principles, rather than to follow them out to their consequences'" (Hamburger, 1999, "There are repeated"). Like Clausewitz, though, Mill was unable to resist giving more detail than he supposed. He has no knowledge of large-scale, strategically planned, public communication but cannot avoid the subject. He takes two positions: proposing a society with constraints on majority public opinion; and equipping individuals to resist received opinion via puffing and newspaper sensationalism.

Constraining popular opinion

What persuasion is allowable to majorities living in liberty and contemplating unpopular minority views? Mill had two maxims. Firstly: "Advice, instruction, persuasion, and avoidance" (Mill, 1977b, "The maxims are"), and secondly subjecting maverick individuals whose views are "prejudicial to the interest of others" to "social or to legal punishments, if society is of opinion that the one or the other is requisite for its protection" (Mill, 1977b, "The maxims are").

The consequences are apparent. In the case of the latter maxim: "Acts injurious to others require a totally different treatment" (Mill, 1977b, "What I contend"). Furthermore: "the dispositions which lead to them, are properly immoral" (Mill, 1977b, "What I contend"). If there is a risk to an individual or the public, "the case is taken out of the province of liberty, and placed in that of morality or law" (Mill, 1977b, "Whenever, in short").

The first maxim covers a greyer area: a person who does no wrong to anyone, but who "may so act as to compel us to judge him", in part to prevent him looking foolish, so "it is doing him a service to warn him of it beforehand". Nor are "we bound to seek his society". We the majority can "caution others against him" and "give others a preference over him in optional good offices, except those which tend to his improvement" (Mill, 1977b, "I do not mean that"). "In these various modes a person may suffer very severe penalties at the hands of others, for faults which concern only himself" (Mill, 1977b, "I do not mean that").

Communicating individuality

Prevention being better than cure, Mill followed Confucius and Plato in looking to the more thoughtful citizens and elaborates on the contents of his earlier "Civilization" essay, to educate citizens for liberty and proof them against media pressure, and the standardization of opinion. To twenty-first-century eyes, much of it resembles a call for greater media literacy. Education at present, Mill warned, promoted assimilation, bringing students access "to the general stock of facts and sentiments", as did faster communication and the rise of manufacturing, and most of all "the ascendancy of public opinion in the State" (Mill, 1977b, "What is it that"). Assimilation means that people:

> [N]ow read the same things, listen to the same things, see the same things, go to the same places, have their hopes and fears directed to the same objects, have the same rights and liberties, and the same means of asserting them.
>
> (Mill, 1977b, "What is it that")

Individualism and education were bulwarks against popular pressure: education, because society has "absolute power over them [weaker individuals] during all the early portion of their existence". Individualism mattered because society has only itself to blame if it "lets any considerable number of its members grow up as mere children":

> [W]hen the opinions of masses of merely average men everywhere become or are becoming the dominant power, the counterpoise and corrective to that tendency would be, the more and more pronounced individuality of those who stand on the higher eminences of thought.
>
> (Mill, 1977b, "I am not countenancing")

"Proofing" the individual

Individuality was "one of the elements of well-being" according to the title of Chapter Three in *On Liberty*, and examples of individual independence must be encouraged and publicized. "It is the duty of governments, and of individuals, to form the truest opinions they can; to form them carefully" (Mill, 1977a, "The objection likely"). "Exceptional individuals, instead of being deterred, should be encouraged in acting differently from the mass" Mill wrote, although "nor is it only persons of decided mental superiority who have a just claim to carry on their own lives in their own way" (Mill, 1977b, "I have said that"). To break through "tyranny of opinion", "people should be eccentric" and "that so few now dare to be eccentric, marks the chief danger of the time" (Mill, 1977b, "In sober truth"). He held up Socrates (Mill, 1977b, "Mankind can hardly") as a famous victim of majority opinion (although the Socrates depicted in *The Republic* shows little interest in protecting the individual from managed public opinion).

Varieties of character were essential. Individual spontaneity and originality must be valued, being at present "no part of the ideal of moral and social reformers" and "rather looked on with jealousy" by them as a "troublesome and perhaps rebellious obstruction" to their plans (Mill, 1977b, "In maintaining this"), which was certainly the case with Plato, al-Farabi, Marx and Engels. In a potentially misleading passage, Mill wrote: "The human faculties of perception, judgement, discriminative feeling, mental activity, and even moral preference, are exercised only in making a choice. He who does everything because it is the custom, makes no choice" (Mill, 1977b, "Little, however, as people").

Mill was not saying custom should always be overthrown. Custom was a valuable guide to experience, but one that should be assessed and interpreted, not automatically copied. The person who simply follows public opinion, "who lets the world, or his portion of it, choose his plan of life for him, has no need of any other faculty than the ape-like one of imitation" (Mill, 1977b, "He who lets"); "has no character, no more than a steam engine has character" (Mill, 1977b, "One whose desires"). "Human nature is not a machine" (Mill, 1977b, "Human nature is"). *On Liberty* makes many pronouncements like these; enough for Milton Friedman to list it as one of his five favourite libertarian books in 2002: "The most concise and clearest statement of the libertarian principle" (Ebenstein, 2012, "Essay Ten").

Education

Individualism must be preserved, and proofed against public opinion management. Compulsory education was the way to do it, not itself liberty but a precondition for it (Mill, 1977b, "These are not questions"). Educating people to be individuals avoided the alternative of a legal system originally designed as a protection, but metamorphosing into a major constraint of liberty. The current generation "is perfectly well able to make the rising generation, as a whole, as good as, and a little better than, itself" (Mill, 1977b, "But I cannot consent").

With the ability to educate, and with the power received wisdom had over weaker minds, "let not society pretend that it needs, besides all this, the power to issue commands and enforce obedience" (Mill, 1977b, "The existing generation is master"). "Is it not almost a self-evident axiom" that the State "should require and compel" the education of its citizens (Mill, 1977b, "Is it not almost")? The education system needs reform. State education "is a mere contrivance for moulding people to be exactly like one another" and "the mould in which it casts them is that which pleases the predominant power in the government" be it monarch, priesthood, aristocracy or "the majority of the existing generation" (Mill, 1977b, "A general State"). "All attempts by the State to bias the conclusions of its citizens on disputed subjects, are evil" (Mill, 1977b, "All attempts by"). If State education should exist at all, it should be "one among many competing experiments, carried on for the purpose of example and stimulus, to keep the others up to a certain standard of excellence" (Mill, 1977b, "A general State").

Public examinations should not measure whether the student has absorbed the values of the majority, but whether "a person possesses the knowledge requisite to make his conclusions, on any different subject, worth attending to" (Mill, 1977b, "All attempts by"). It is part of the "political education of a free people", exposing them to influences outside family, to joint interests and managing joint concerns, "habituating them to act from public or semi-public motives" and "guide their conduct by aims which unite" instead of isolate (Mill, 1977b, "The second objection").

Mill's "Civilization" essay concentrated on the universities, to achieve "the regeneration of individual character among our lettered and opulent classes" (Mill, 1977a, "These things must bide"). It advocated more classics and logic, and less training "in the business of the world" whose empirical knowledge properly educated persons would in any case acquire easily, and more critically (Mill, 1977a, "We would have classics"):

> [The] corner-stone of an education intended to form great minds ... is to
> call forth the greatest possible quantity of intellectual power, and to

inspire the intensest love of truth: and this without a particle of regard to the results to which the exercise of that power may lead.

(Mill, 1977a, "The very corner-stone")

Puffery, public opinion, majority pressure and government acquiescence: Mill identified several ingredients of a communication revolution that undermined liberty. Citizens must be able to stand above the commercial and political hubbub, judge it independently, and set its competing claims in proportion. One hundred and fifty years later, can it be said this has been achieved?

On Liberty advocated an entire social system that resisted outright puffing, and publicity's social pressures. It must be said that there are many omissions; inevitable because of the time it was written. Hamburger and Himmelfarb rightly see it in part as an attempt to control the majority, and the long-term consequences of that for social unity and cooperation were secondary to the main task. Mill saw the changes coming over "public opinion" but not how the management of communication was evolving, or how intricate and creative it would become beginning in the America he admired, perhaps to overcome the extreme individuality of the citizens Mill praised. He saw the rise of powerful media platforms and the receptiveness of a more literate population to organized, communicated opinion; but not the incredible volume of managed communication that made it hard for the most individual of individuals to resist. This essay was after all a proposal for withstanding, not using managed public communication.

On Liberty is concerned with popular communication's effect on us as individuals and not as members of a group. Surely this concern is justified today when individuals are gathered into groups, categorized, organized, coalesced and reconstituted, and where the numerical balance of minorities and majorities is exploited by PR practitioners. Mill's ideas for proofing society against these activities help us see where *On Liberty's* general prescriptions would lead. It does come close to an ideal in which managed public communication is at least supervised, and individualism nurtured. What though happens if the best educated themselves use "puffery" to gain their objectives? Can, for example, the "one per cent" subvert the perceptions of the ninety nine per cent? Mill is setting limits on what the majority can do, but not on what individuals should do to fairly communicate opinion. In *On Liberty* Mill supposed cultivating individualism among "the herd" would address his problem. Educated individuals would be more discriminating, fair-minded, and virtuous in their publicity. Unlike Confucius, Plato and al-Farabi he did not ask what would happen if they were not.

References

Ebenstein, L. (2012) *The Indispensable Milton Friedman: Essays on Politics and Economics.* New York: Regnery Publishing.

Hamburger, J. (1999) *John Stuart Mill on Liberty and Control.* Princeton, NJ: Princeton University Press.

Hayek, F. A. (2007) *The Road to Serfdom: Text and Documents.* Edited by B. Caldwell. Chicago, IL: University of Chicago Press.

Himmelfarb, G. (2006) *The Moral Imagination: From Edmund Burke to Lionel Trilling.* Chicago, IL: Ivan R. Dee.

Jacobson, D. (2000) "Mill on Liberty, Speech, and the Free Society." *Philosophy & Public Affairs,* 29(3): 276–309.

Kafka, F. (1983) *The Complete Stories.* Edited by N. N. Glatzer. Foreword by J. Updike. New York: Schocken Books.

Kierkegaard, S. (2009) *The Crowd is Untruth.* Translated by C. Bellinger. New York: Vanessa Myers.

Le Bon, G. (2001) *The Crowd: A Study of the Popular Mind.* Mineola, NY: Dover Publications.

Liberal Democrat History Group (2009) *Great Liberals.* Retrieved from www.liberal history.org.uk/item_single.php?item_id=110&item=history.

Marx, K. (1990) *Capital: A Critique of Political Economy.* Translated by B. Fowkes. London: Penguin Books in association with New Left Review.

Mill, J. S. (1977a) "Civilization". In *The Collected Works of John Stuart Mill,* Volume XVIII. Edited by J. M. Robson. Introduction by A. Brady. Toronto: University of Toronto Press, London: Routledge and Kegan Paul. Retrieved from http://oll.liberty fund.org/?option=com_staticxt& staticfile=show.php%3Fcollection=46&Itemid=27.

——(1977b) "On Liberty." In *The Collected Works of John Stuart Mill,* Volume XVIII. Edited by J. M. Robson. Introduction by A. Brady. Toronto: University of Toronto Press, London: Routledge and Kegan Paul. Retrieved from http://oll.libertyfund.org/ ?option=com_staticxt&staticfile=show.php%3Fcollection=46&Itemid=27.

——(1977c) "Considerations on Representative Government." In *The Collected Works of John Stuart Mill, Volume XIX—Essays on Politics and Society [1859]. Part 2.* Edited by A. P. and J. M. Robson. Introduction by A. Brady. Toronto: University of Toronto Press, London: Routledge and Kegan Paul. Retrieved from http://oll.liberty fund.org/?option=com_staticxt&staticfile=show.php%3Fcollection=46&Itemid=27.

——(1981) "Autobiography." In *The Collected Works of John Stuart Mill, Volume I— Autobiography and Literary Essays [1824].* Edited by J. M. Robson and J. Stillinger. Introduction by Lord Robbins. Toronto: University of Toronto Press, London: Routledge and Kegan Paul. Retrieved from http://oll.libertyfund.org/?option= com_staticxt&staticfile=show.php%3Fcollection=46&Itemid=27.

——(1984) "Review of Austin's Lectures on Jurisprudence (1832)." In *The Collected Works of John Stuart Mill, Volume XXI—Essays on Equality, Law, and Education [1825].* Edited by J. M. Robson. Introduction by S. Collini. Toronto: University of Toronto Press, London: Routledge and Kegan Paul. Retrieved from http://oll.liberty fund.org/?option=com_staticxt&staticfile=show.php%3Fcollection=46&Itemid=27.

——(1985) "Utilitarianism." In *The Collected Works of John Stuart Mill, Volume X— Essays on Ethics, Religion, and Society [1833].* Edited by J. M. Robson, Introduction by F. E. L. Priestley. Toronto: University of Toronto Press, London: Routledge and Kegan Paul. Retrieved from http://oll.libertyfund.org/?option=com_staticxt& staticfile=show.php%3Fcollection=46&Itemid=27.

——(1986a) *The Collected Works of John Stuart Mill, Volume XXII—Newspaper Writings December 1822–July 1831, Part I [1822].* Edited by A. P. and J. M. Robson. Introduction by A. P. Robson and J. M. Robson. Toronto: University of

Toronto Press, London: Routledge and Kegan Paul. Retrieved from http://oll.liberty fund.org/?option=com_staticxt&staticfile=show.php%3Fcollection=46&Itemid=27.

——(1986b) *The Collected Works of John Stuart Mill, Volume XXV—Newspaper Writings December 1847–July 1873, Part IV [1847].* Edited by A. P. and J. M. Robson. Introduction by A. P. Robson and J. M. Robson. Toronto: University of Toronto Press, London: Routledge and Kegan Paul. Retrieved from http://oll.liberty fund.org/?option=com_staticxt&staticfile=show.php%3Fcollection=46&Itemid=27.

Russell, B. (1961) *History of Western Philosophy and its Connection with Circum-stances from the Earliest Times to Present Day.* London: Routledge.

Wiland, E. (2001) "Book Review of Joseph Hamburger, John Stuart Mill on Liberty and Control". *Ethics,* 111(3): 637–38.

9 Modern campaign management?

Mohandas (Mahatma) Ghandi (1869–1948), *Autobiography: The Story of my Experiments with Truth* (1925–29)

Gandhi and PR: Mobilizing symbolism

Is it possible that a book listed as one of the most spiritual books of the twentieth century is also a guide to PR? The list was created by a panel for *USA Today* and Harpers San Francisco and naturally has its own practical PR value, but the reader might not expect the inclusion of a work so attentive to the mechanics of managed communication, and one with a thoroughly modern grip on the topic (USA Today, 1999). It must once again be remembered that spirituality need not ignore operational practicalities.

Gandhi's *Autobiography* appeared in weekly instalments between 1925 and 1929, and was first published in two volumes in 1927 and 1929, during his temporary retreat from public life. It is a rich fusion of spirituality, politics, dietetics, his behaviour towards his wife, celibacy and an approach to ritual and belief according more with the *Analects* than *The Republic*, the whole amounting to a struggle for self-mastery by Gandhi who wrestled as much against personal temptations as with social injustice in South Africa and India. It is a contrasting blend of approaches, perhaps due to its origins as articles. Parts of it are as frank as St Augustine's troubled *Confessions*; as serene as portions of the *Analects*; as reasoned as *On Liberty* and turbulent as Luther or *The Communist Manifesto*. All of these elements are apparent in Gandhi's Introduction, in which he writes:

> I hope to acquaint the reader fully with all my faults and errors … For it is an unbroken torture to me that I am still so far from Him, who, as I fully know, governs every breath of my life, and whose offspring I am.
>
> (Gandhi, 2008, "I hope and pray that")

Gandhi showed a surer knowledge of publicity:

> He was able to arouse three hundred and twenty million people to political consciousness, whereas a large number of politicians and patriots, endowed with perhaps greater powers of intellect, had failed to touch the masses, except for a small fringe.
>
> (Motvani, 1930, p. 574)

This was the judgement of a contemporary Indian observer, in a fascinating academic paper on Gandhi's "propaganda" (a catch-all phrase for all managed public communication often used at that time, for government and non-government publicity, as already described in this book). The British Movie-tone newsreel company captured his alertness to publicity when a subsidiary visited his Indian Ashram in 1931 and became possibly the first media outlet to record his voice. He is being interviewed by an American journalist who— banal sign of celebrity status—is principally interested in Gandhi's choice of clothing if he attends the British-Indian Conference in London. Sitting on the ground, clad in a dhoti, at one point opening and reading a letter, Gandhi is asked if he would wear traditional Indian clothes to visit the King. Gandhi hesitantly and briefly answers: "In any other dress I should be most dis-courteous to him, because I should be artificial" (British Movietone, 1931, 2:43). Gandhi had already written in the *Autobiography*: "my constitutional shyness has been no disadvantage whatever. In fact I can see that, on the contrary, it has been all to my advantage" (Gandhi, 2008, "I must say that"). One of those advantages, "economy of words", was certainly suited to the age of newsreels, radio interviews and newspaper reporting.

Autobiography contemplates the themes raised in the short newsreel, all of which made the Mahatma "an innovative technician of mass publicity" (Mazzarella, 2010, p. 1). At the same time, the spiritual power of Gandhi resembles that of Confucius to the point where, it is noted: "In many Indian homes the pictures of Lord Krishna and Gandhi are hanging side by side" (Balaram, 1989, p. 70). In his "experiments" are found the themes of truth, authenticity, spirituality, sincerity, the search for the Divine; the whole amounting to a lean medieval aestheticism combined with a very modern use of public campaign techniques. *Autobiography* is part-autobiography, part social-analysis, and part guidebook for the organization of popular opi-nion. One part cannot be understood without reference to the other two, and today this is a characteristic of campaign-based PR, and the goal of much other PR besides. Its purpose is to ensure that a message is absorbed into the beliefs and emotions of the targeted audiences, and if possible to connect the smallest of clients, products or causes to universal social values. This is what Gandhi achieved, issue after issue, campaign by campaign, showing a talent for campaign mobilization few have matched. Gandhi, furthermore, *became* the message, managing to embody it so completely that it achieved a strong degree of spirituality that added authenticity to his campaigns. Marx's strictly economic explanation for the true fetishism of the commodity is baffled by Gandhi, whose value has been lent to a special edition Montblanc luxury pen, along with a host of other consumer items conjuring, it is claimed, "a zone of divine and market logics" (Khanduri, 2012, p. 303). And yet what seems apparent and inevitable to the student of public relations may not be to others. Gandhi made symbolic PR use of more everyday artefacts himself: the dhoti, the spinning wheel, salt. "He wanted", pointed out a contemporary, "to turn the nation's suppressed wrath against the agents of tyranny toward the things that perpetuated its slavery" (Motvani, 1930, p. 577).

Gandhi's symbolic PR was enmeshed with his spirituality and his techniques have become standard for many subsequent campaigns: "The briefest examination of nonviolent action reveals that communication is essential to its effectiveness" (Martin & Varney, 2003, p. 213), and communication will not stay within prescribed or preferred boundaries; it will take the cause and the participants far from their original intention, if the audiences and communication technology wills it. So it was with Gandhi, and the ideas he developed and later set down in *Autobiography*.

To understand what Gandhi has to say about PR—and now we are moving into something recognizable as modern PR—it seems essential to understand what his approach reminds us about PR in general, namely that it is where organizations encounter the wider world, and the larger hopes, fears and in both cases feelings of individuals and communities. The heart of the function cannot be expressed by statistics, self-defeating scholarly models, and micromeasurement or in the workings of software and social media. These are occasionally important, transient tools. Gandhi knew that connecting with humanity required humanity, and something deeper still. In *The Origins of Knowledge and Imagination* (1979) a republished Yale lecture series, the mathematician and biologist Jacob Bronowski suggested:

> [W]e would not really want as human beings to do science or mathematics if we were thereby forbidden to think about ourselves, to talk about ourselves, and to compare our feelings from the inside with what we suppose other people to feel whom we only view from the outside.
>
> (Bronowski, 1979, p. 98)

If this view has validity for high mathematics how much more valid it is for "lowlier" PR. It is not valid to exclude self-reference or self-consciousnessness, or reference to emotion in a field that depends on it, on the grounds that unlike, for instance, Trevelyan's atom (see Chapter One), they are "scientifically" hard to isolate. The place of these forces in PR scholarship has not been sufficiently explored. An effective way of doing so may be to study the history of movements, social aspirations and of ideas for organizing society. Gandhi was active in all three, and this is one of the reasons for his personal effectiveness as a public communicator, and as the organizer of communication-intensive campaigns. In recent years PR has flourished on the back of society's rising interest in these and other kinds of self-regard, with more ways of expressing it.

There are larger aspects of Gandhi's work that must be recorded here for their relevance to his PR activities. For many years, almost up to the *Autobiography's* publication, he did not seek India's independence from the British Empire, but independence within it. Gandhi wrote of his years in South

Africa: "Hardly ever have I known anybody to cherish such loyalty as I did to the British Constitution. I can see now that my love of truth was at the root of this loyalty" (Gandhi, 2008, "Hardly ever have I"). There was much about the relationship between Britain and India he valued, and with more imagination than generations of imperial officials, he saw the potential of a global community of independent states within a shared framework. Several of his formative decisions were taken after reading British authors—Henry Salt's *Plea for Vegetarianism* (1886), John Ruskin's *Unto this Last* (1860)—that Gandhi felt connected the public work for the greater good to knowledge that "the life of the tiller or soil and the handicraftsman, is the life worth living" (Gandhi, 2008, "I believe that I discovered"). Gandhi tried blending this last point into his life and work, by spinning, and living and working in ashrams, conveying a spiritually sincere personality that added to the effectiveness of his PR. Second, Gandhi developed his talent for large-scale issues campaigns in different countries for different issues: vegetarianism in the UK, the treatment of Indian laborers in South Africa, and the status of the untouchables in India, with each campaign escalating in scale from the one before. At each stage, Gandhi learned valuable lessons about organizing publicity, including leafleting and press relations, event planning, and investing his activities with a personal sincerity that for some transcended worldly affairs and made him an internationally known figure. Both factors, imperial and local community activism, taught Gandhi the value of campaigns that were local and global, as many issues management campaigns are today, which finally outgrew imperialism itself. *Autobiography* itself was composed before his 1930 civil disobedience campaigns brought him world attention. Between 1924 and 1929 Gandhi focused on local not global activities. "Gandhi retreated from the political arena, emphasizing grassroots constructive work, instead of dramatic direct action" (Chabot and Duyvendak, 2002, p. 710).

The book blends local and global values with the author's spiritual journey. There is ample material for a PR cynic, for instance in the Introduction: "for me, truth is the sovereign principle, which includes numerous other principles"—truth in word, in thought, the "relative truth of our conception" and "the Absolute Truth, the Eternal Principle, that is God" (Gandhi, 2008, "If I had only"). It is hard to imagine a twenty-first-century guide to PR being quite so daring, or self-regarding. It is not clear if Gandhi fully achieved Truth, but many at least believed he came very close. This aspiration must be kept in mind, as it informs Gandhi's "account of various practical applications of those principles" (Gandhi, 2008, "If I had only") that deserve attention, for he enlarges upon the individuality advocated by Mill, recognizes its rich spirituality which Mill the former utilitarian does not, and demonstrates how spiritually motivated individuals can cooperate as a large group to bring change. Gandhi's autobiography explains how to campaign as a union of autonomous individuals, rather than (unlike Marx and Engels) subsuming individuality into a monolithic mass for a common cause. It is advocacy PR for a self-regarding age, an age of mechanization whose inhabitants—knowingly or not—are seeking a spiritual centre. Balaram compares Ghandi's songs, prayers, clothing, adoption of the spinning wheel as a symbol of independence, and other characteristics with those attributed to the deity Krishna: "Unquestionably, Gandhi's popularity with the masses is attributable largely to his use of symbols and rhetorical devices that have their origin in Indian mythology and popular culture" (Balaram, 1989, p. 72).

This was powerful PR—and it must be stressed to any non-specialist readers that linking his name with that function is neither cynical or pejorative—and more participatory than any earlier techniques, although those techniques also remain in use. The spinning wheel campaign came to symbolize India's self-sufficiency and independence from British manufactories, and looked to supply spinning wheels that created employment. It was conducted communally for and by peasants using "intense propaganda", largely educational. Gandhi's Ashram became "a veritable training institution for spinners, weavers and carders" (Motvani, 1930, p. 576). Competitions were organized, bonfires made of foreign clothing, and rich people were asked to "give up their foreign clothes" (Motvani, 1930, p. 576). There was, Motvani declares, "no 'viciousness'" attached to Gandhi's propaganda (Motvani, 1930, p. 576). This must be said clearly for more than one reason, because it also reminds us of a well-known and dangerous tendency among non-practitioners today to separate out any public communication activities they do agree with, from activities they not agree with, and describe the latter practices as mere "public relations" or "propaganda" without realizing PR is directing *all* the communication activities they are exposed to (Martin and Varney, 2003, pp. 213, 230).

Clarifying an identity

One practical principle came to unite the whole in the world of public affairs, and galvanized audiences around the world. This is described in Chapter twenty-four of *Autobiography*, in a passage that throws incidental light on Gandhi's other PR skills. The principle itself evolved during his South African campaigns and became known in English as "passive resistance" but Gandhi felt that term "was too narrowly construed, that it was supposed to be a weapon of the weak, that it could be characterized by hatred, and that it could finally manifest itself as violence" (Gandhi, 2008, "Events were so shaping"). Recognizing the power of a phrase to clarify, simplify, characterize and motivate, it "was clear that a new word must be coined by the Indians to designate their struggle".

Gandhi could not think of one himself, and displaying his head for publicity ran a newspaper competition for the best suggestion. The final choice, slightly amended by Gandhi, was "Satygraha", or as he translated it "Truth Firmness" (Gandhi, 2008, "As a result Maganlal"). The term and techniques it embodied spread to India, and to other movements worldwide, as Gandhi continued applying it as part of his experiments with truth in private and public life, integrating the cause, the spiritual quest, modern communication and individual aspirations.

Gandhi also benefited from the global communication opportunities presented by the British Empire, partly stemming from the simple fact that a public campaign against an injustice in one part of the Empire sometimes had to attract attention in other parts. One of his first campaigns was against a tax on Indian indentured workers brought to South Africa to serve on sugar cane plantations, who settled in the country once their indenture ended and became very effective business competitors with local Europeans. Many of his local campaigns had such imperial ramifications, attracting publicity in the UK, India, and elsewhere in the Empire, as well as South Africa. The disfranchising campaign in Natal taught Gandhi that "sustained agitation was essential for making an impression on the Secretary of State for the Colonies" which resulted in the creation of the Natal Indian Congress for conducting it (Gandhi, 2008, "Practice as a lawyer").

Gandhi, and PR as "public work"

Gandhi often described his legal-civil-campaigning activities as "public work", which is to say it was an intensified version of Mill's newspaper publicity to educate public opinion, initially emerging in the educational activities of groups like the Vegetarian Society in the UK, to which Gandhi belonged, and—in almost the same period—public campaigns against the plutocrats of America's "Gilded Age". It intensified as Gandhi's work became more political, whether advocating for vegetarianism in London's Bayswater district or for the Indian community in Natal, or later Indian independence. The "public work" he helped develop had operational characteristics that resemble those of today's issues-based non-profit PR. It had legal objectives, which necessitated press relations. It was also educational, which necessitated community and publishing initiatives. It had legislative and political requirements, which were assisted by encouraging mass mobilization through petitions, speaking tours, media coverage of staged events. Gandhi's campaigns publicized its leaders and emphasized simple principles, which helped to give the movement a clear identity that could be energetically promoted and distributed, part of the process already described by which Gandhi himself in his lifetime took on a near-divine status among some audiences. Confucius only experienced this apotheosis posthumously, if only because his followers lacked a fast and comprehensive way to spread their message. Luther's earthier spirituality attracted similar attention, if not quite so fully realized or carefully managed.

Gandhi learned the value of large-scale publicity activities in South Africa. Local Indian protest at exclusion from the South Africa's 1894 Natal Franchise Bill, for instance, led to a "monster petition" that allowed activists to carry the message to villages across the Province, and was used as a publicity vehicle in India as well as South Africa. Gandhi: "sent copies to all the newspapers and publicists I knew" in India; other copies "were sent to journals and publicists in England representing different parties. The London *Times* supported our claims" (Gandhi, 2008, "The petition was at last"). Here, as shall be shown elsewhere, Gandhi realized the PR value of an item went beyond its ostensible function. That item could just as well be material like a petition, or non-material like "Satygraha". The petition for instance had multiple communication advantages: it influenced political and non-political audiences; the act of preparing it could be publicized, and reporting its progress created other communication opportunities; the task of distributing it generated yet more, and spread the message to further-flung audiences and media outlets if the news and distribution was well handled. New audiences might be mobilized and new pressures placed on key decision-makers.

Gandhi founded the Natal Indian Congress in 1894 to organize a public work effort, and *Autobiography* offers still-helpful advice firstly about managing funds; secondly, about helping and bringing target audiences together in meetings, the media and via a small library, to build a common agenda and political identity. "The third feature of the Congress was propaganda" which in this instance reached international audiences, consisting of "acquainting the English in South Africa and England and people in India with the real state of things in Natal" (Gandhi, 2008, "The third feature"). Congress also took care to communicate in the voice of their target audiences: "The use of traditional idioms and local dialects in its propaganda is notable" (Pandey, 1975, p. 207).

Gandhi managed much of his private and public life in terms of its impact on public reputation. He displayed far more awareness of the self-discipline this required than most public figures. This followed an early lesson: Gandhi had missed a badly incorrect estimate on the profitability of *Indian Opinion*, and learned "that a public worker should not make statements of which he has not made sure" (Gandhi, 2008, "I now realize that"). It was a mix of principle, self-questioning, and political awareness that led Gandhi to alter his style of dress in South Africa "so as to make it more in keeping with that of the indentured labourers." Returning to India, he "invested in an eight-to-ten annas Kashmiri cap. One dressed in that fashion was sure to pass muster as a poor man" (Gandhi, 2008, "During the Satygraha"). Once more, spirituality, *Realpolitik* and personal sincerity intensified the impact of his public communication.

Pamphlets, letters, inquiries

Gandhi was not a ready public speaker; sometimes others read out his speeches for him. His talent was for writing. He and those who worked with him wrote many materials for his campaigns, and again he understood their wider potential as publicity tools. They were usually his first step when confronting any issue. The launch of the Natal Congress was followed in 1895 by two pamphlets, "An appeal to every Briton in South Africa" and "The Indian Franchise—an appeal". One of the most effective pamphlets describing South

African conditions was written and self-published in India in 1896, and later became famous as the "Green Pamphlet", because of its cover. Gandhi recollected that: "Ten thousand copies were printed and (with the help of local schoolchildren) posted to all the papers and leaders of every party in India" (Gandhi, 2008, "I went straight to Rajkot"). Aside from being covered by Indian newspapers, it was picked up by the news agency Reuters and a three-line version cabled to London, and thence to South Africa. The reaction certainly exposed him to the challenge of managing increased volumes of information at high speed, because the Reuter cable acted like Bismarck's Ems telegram, creating "a miniature, but exaggerated, edition of the picture I had drawn of the treatment accorded to the Indians in Natal, and it was not in my words" (Gandhi, 2008, "I went straight to Rajkot").

Pamphlet sales were supported by publicity for the author's public appearances, and speeches in the wake of related events. One such was the beating of an indentured Indian servant in Durban, South Africa, by his well-known European master. Gandhi's Madras speech on the outrage was printed and "at the close of the meeting there was a regular run on the 'Green Pamphlet'" leading to a second revised edition which "sold like hot cakes" (Gandhi, 2008, "I next proceeded to Madras").

Letters to the press were also used to publicize Gandhi's positions, for instance on the neglect of Black Plague victims by the Municipality of Johannesburg. It could dangerously backfire. When he returned to South Natal in time for the opening of the new Parliament, Gandhi announced it to the Indian Press, and arrived to a near-lynching in Durban.

The value of investigative research is well known in PR today. The Natal and the Indian Congress parties, encouraged by Gandhi, made excellent use of inquiries as a means to attract support and publicize abuses, as the inquiry proceeded and when it finally reported. In India Gandhi conducted one on the indigo farmer's tax. Congress made non-official inquiries into the 1920 Jallianwala Bagh (Amritsar) massacre, which broadened the issue into the competence of colonial administration to check abuse, and built the reputation of the Congress Party from an organization that "would meet three days every year and then go to sleep" into one that took India into Independence (Gandhi, 2008, "I made friends with"). "[A] flood of nationalist pamphlets, leaflets, posters and the like" appeared after the launch of the Congress civil disobedience campaign, starting with Gandhi's salt march in 1930, a year after the second and final volume of *Autobiography* was published (Pandey, 1975, p. 211).

Media relations

With the means to inspire large numbers of largely illiterate people into action (and communication), it hardly needs saying that the press was not "the sole, or even the chief, agency employed by Congress for the purposes of propaganda or mobilization" (Pandey, 1975, p. 206). That said, the episode of the Movietone newsreel interview shows Gandhi knew the national and global advantages of working with the media, and mastered or used his shyness to project simplicity, strength, authenticity and likability. A sentence appears in Gandhi's *Autobiography* that might easily have been written by Mill: "The newspaper press is a great power, but just as an unchained torrent of water submerges whole countrysides and devastates crops, even so an uncontrolled pen serves but to destroy" (Gandhi, 2008, "In the very first month"). "The useful and the useless must, like good and evil generally, go on together" concludes Gandhi, again in the spirit of Mill, "and man must make his choice" (Gandhi, 2008, "In the very first"). *Autobiography* describes his developing contacts with journalists and editors on South African affairs, with whom he regularly seemed to become "acquainted", meeting for instance with the *Daily Telegraph* representative in Calcutta's Bengal Club, who then discovers what Gandhi doubtless anticipated or suspected, that Indians were barred from the Club drawing-room (Gandhi, 2008, "From Madras I proceeded). He called at newspaper offices with varying degrees of success (according to Gandhi the editor of *The Bangabasi,* among India's most respected and nationalist newspapers of the day told him, "There is no end to the number of visitors like you. You had better go" [Gandhi, 2008, "I saw that my task"]). More productive meetings were held with Anglo-Indian editors. One of these, the editor of *The Englishman,* gave Gandhi office space and the liberty of editing his leading article on the Natal problem. The editor of *The Madras Standard* "often invited me to his office and gave me guidance", and "placed the columns of *The Madras Standard* entirely at my disposal, and I freely availed myself of the offer". *The Hindu* representatives "also were very sympathetic" (Gandhi, 2008, "The greatest help"). Not that Gandhi restricted his media work to newspapers and readers most likely to sympathize. Imaginatively, he "wanted to secure the help of every party" and for that reason met with the editor of *The Pioneer,* who "promised to notice anything in the paper that I might write" on South Africa, adding "that he could not promise to endorse all the Indian demands". "It is enough", Gandhi sensibly replied, "that you should study the question and discuss it in your paper". Publicity could be useful in its own right, whatever its perspective (Gandhi, 2008, "I took a room").

There is an impressive alertness about Gandhi's management of the temperature and tone of public coverage. One of the earliest acts of Satygraha in India was in 1917 and 1919, over the refusal to pay tax by starving peasants in the Champaran district of Bihar, who were forced by planters to grow indigo and not food. Gandhi realized that it should be dealt with separately from the issue of Indian independence, to avoid changing Government neutrality to active hostility: "So I wrote to the editors of the principal papers requesting them not to trouble to send any reporters, as I should send them whatever might be necessary for publication and keep them informed" (Gandhi, 2008, "Indeed the situation in"), and then "sent to the leaders and the principal papers occasional reports, not for publication, but merely for their information" (Gandhi, 2008, "In such a delicate"). Issue-by-issue, campaign-by-campaign communication that cumulatively points to a shared overall objective remains a popular technique.

In South Africa Gandhi controlled and helped fund the newspaper *Indian Opinion* launched in 1904. "Satygraha would probably have been impossible without *Indian Opinion*" he reflected (Gandhi, 2008, "But after all these years"). Later in India he became editor of *Young India* and *Navagjivan*. He did not run advertisements in these two papers, a step "that has in no small measure helped them to maintain their independence", and of course "enabled me freely to ventilate my views and to put heart into the people" (Gandhi, 2008, "From the very start"). The activities of the Indian Congress after 1930 generated many short-lived periodicals for the cause, again "often in the rural dialect of a region, rather than the khari boli of the educated towns-folk. There was no other way of speaking to the masses" (Pandey, 1975, p. 216). It is noteworthy evidence of targeting audiences like "brother cultivators" (Pandey, 1975, p. 222), a method, if not directly suggested by Gandhi, which certainly evolved because he adopted and publicized the symbols popular with the poor. "Service of the poor", he wrote, "has been my heart's desire, and it has always thrown me amongst the poor and enabled me to identify myself with them" (Gandhi, 2008, "The heart's earnest"). He reinvigorated the publicity of the Indian Congress; and it began targeting previously neglected audiences: "Other publications singled out other groups, e.g. shopkeepers, launderers, barbers, in one case, and factory workers, in another" (Pandey, 1975, p. 216).

"I must reduce myself to zero" wrote Gandhi near the end of *Autobiography* (Gandhi, 2008, "The experiences and experiments"). He lamented his failure to do so, and this failure was certainly apparent in his campaigns, which made him into a global personality. The attention he attracted was partly because of his much-publicized struggle for personal purity and *Ahimsa*, or non-hurting, non-violence in all forms, not only political. The public campaigns he led were in the end sanctified by his personal embodiment of his public work. To many people, that personal search for the Truth validated his public search for Truth through non-violence. Today, Gandhi remains "the most prominent figure in this tradition" (Martin and Varney, 2003, p. 214). *Autobiography* is a guide for socially aware PR today, and for a communication philosophy many commercial, political and nonprofit organizations seek to replicate. The approach identifies a cause target audiences instinctively believe to be genuine because its representatives seem to have sincere convictions, seem to be incorruptible. They have also created a clearly identifiable organization for conducting their campaign, defined a simple series of goals orbiting round a universal value. They are able to relate those goals to local events, people or issues, to back their cause with research and investigation, non-violent expressions of dissent, and to publicize it with the creative use of media. *Autobiography* describes all these facets of modern issues-based PR, which inspired many imitators, some more genuine than others. Possibly the communication world is now choked to distraction by such activities, adapted but not reinvented for new technologies. It is possible that a new Gandhi, seeking to change the individual and a society, will in doing so refresh PR once again.

References

Balaram, S. (1989) "Product Symbolism of Gandhi and its Connection with Indian Mythology." *Design Issues,* 5(2): 68–85.

British Movietone. (1931) *Gandhi is Persuaded to Talk!* Newsreel. Retrieved from www.youtube.com/watch?v=jY9Avdn2Z38.

Bronowski, J. (1979) *The Origins of Knowledge and Imagination.* New Haven, CT: Yale University Press.

Chabot, S. and Duyvendak, J. W. (2002) "Globalization and Transnational Diffusion between Social Movements: Reconceptualizing the Dissemination of the Gandhian Repertoire and the 'Coming Out' Routine." *Theory and Society,* 31(6): 697–740.

Gandhi. (2008) *Autobiography: The Story of my Experiments with Truth.* Thousand Oaks, CA: BN Publishing.

Khanduri, Ritu Gairola (2012) "Some Things about Gandhi." *Contemporary South Asia,* 20(3): 303–25.

Martin, B. and Varney, W. (2003) "Nonviolence and Communication." *Journal of Peace Research,* 40(2): 213–32.

Mazzarella, W. (2010) "Branding the Mahatma: The Untimely Provocation of Gandhian Publicity." *Cultural Anthropology,* 25(1): 1–39.

Motvani, K. L. (1930) "Propaganda in Mahatma Gandhi's Movement." *Social Forces,* 8(4): 574–81.

Pandey, G. (1975) "Mobilization in a Mass Movement: Congress 'Propaganda' in the United Provinces (India), 1930–34." *Modern Asian Studies,* 9(2): 205–26.

USA Today (1999) "Spiritual Books of the Century." *USA Today.* December 2. Retrieved from http://usatoday30.usatoday.com/life/enter/books/book372.htm.

10 Accepting and fearing PR

Friedrich von Hayek (1899–1992),
The Road to Serfdom (1944)

"Propaganda" in *The Road to Serfdom*

In *The Road to Serfdom* Mill's concern for the majority's hold over publicity becomes Hayek's concern for publicity's hold over the majority. "This is a political book" the economist Hayek wrote in his original Preface. It was political because it reminded wartime public opinion about the virtues of classical liberalism and its place in post-war policy, and not only economic policy. The thrust of the book, in the neat sentences of one reviewer, denied that Germans were naturally "vicious" and traced "the growth of totalitarianism back to the insidious growth of the philosophies in which the urge to 'plan', in its modern connotation, is rooted" (Fisher, 1944, p. 415).

This was the original reason for Hayek's interest in "propaganda" as he, Gandhi, Bernays and many others called managed public communication, before the word was reserved for darker purposes. Much of *The Road to Serfdom*, either as text or sub-text, grapples with the effect certain kinds of large-scale public communication was having on opinion, and the need for alternative messages. His mentor, the fellow-Austrian economist Ludwig von Mises (1881–1973) who had been instrumental in leading Hayek from democratic socialism, may have influenced Hayek on this also. Mises had written a "Critique of the doctrine of force" in his *Liberalism, in the classical tradition* (1927): "Whoever wants to see the world governed according to his own ideas must strive for dominion over men's minds" adding "Men cannot be made happy against their will" (Mises, 1927, Chapter 1, Section 9). True Liberalism, he wrote, must "eschew every trick of propaganda" (Mises, 1927, Appendix, Section 2). What then could it do, and what counted as a "trick"?

Hayek was more open to propaganda; in fact he wanted to do it, writing to the British Ministry of Information on the outbreak of war in 1939 "offering to aid with any propaganda campaign that might be directed at the German-speaking countries". He submitted a series of proposals for delivering the message, based on an historical interpretation of German thought and politics. In the introduction to the 2007 edition of *The Road to Serfdom*, Caldwell says the offer was turned down "politely but firmly"—and certainly unimaginatively, given that this approach later resurfaced in Allied propaganda (Hayek, 2007, "Hayek had sent").

Hayek gave thought to what propaganda counted as valid, and what messages were worth communicating, and his views led to *The Road to Serfdom.* An interest in "blatant" and "subtle" forms of propaganda by the immediate enemy, National Socialist Germany, as "one of his main weapons" appears throughout *The Road to Serfdom* (Hayek, 2007, "It is still more"). Hayek criticized the "fatuous ineffectiveness of most British propaganda" and worried about what it implied: "[T]hose directing it seem to have lost their own belief in the peculiar values of English civilization or to be completely ignorant of the main points on which it differs from that of other people" (Hayek, 2007, "Nowhere is the loss").

Britain's countering message "that we are fighting for freedom to shape our life according to our own ideas" while important, was "not enough to give us the firm beliefs which we need" (Hayek, 2007, "We know that we"). This interest in communication management raised two further questions for Hayek—what should those firm beliefs be, and who else threatens freedom by opposing, forgetting or overlooking them? He was concerned for the future of classical free market liberal society in the communication climate being created so his answers were, first, believe in economic liberalism and second, that the threat to freedom came from all proponents of state intervention in the economy. Economically speaking National Socialists, Communists and socialist socialists looked similar. One position in his book was that Nazism, in the words of one critic, "has its roots in the teachings and doctrines of German Socialists" (Hoselitz, 1945, p. 929). Also blamed were the "Left intelligentsia" in Britain who "seem to have become almost incapable of seeing any good in the characteristic English institutions and traditions" (Hayek, 2007, "The Left intelligentsia"). Hayek added others to the Charge Sheet, dedicating the book to "The socialists of all parties". These evidently included monopoly capitalists who cooperated with the State to protect and grow their position, influencing public opinion "by letting other groups participate in their gains ... or, and perhaps even more frequently, by persuading them that the formation of monopolies was in the public interest" (Hayek, 2007, "In some measure").

Hayek, the Austrian in voluntary exile had seen the process unfold in Germany: the weakening of a free economy by the Left, leading to a weakening of public respect for free institutions, leading to the rise of extreme nationalist collectivism, and yet as he afterwards recalled there were people "seriously believing that National Socialism was a capitalist reaction against socialism" (Hayek, 2007, "A very special situation"). Had Britain unwittingly fallen for this error and thus embarked down the same path? "We shall not persuade them [the German people] by following them half the way which leads to totalitarianism" and we will ultimately undermine our own freedom by borrowed German ideas about "state socialism, Realpolitik, 'scientific' planning, or corporativism" (Hayek, 2007, "We shall not delude").

These were the reasons for his book: to counter the wider statist, collectivist source of what he called "totalitarian propaganda" (whose methods still appear in PR or specifically Issues or Public Affairs PR), that looked to continue this statist, collectivist threat to liberty into the post-war period. "For more than half a century," he had written in 1935:

> [T]he belief that deliberate regulation of all social affairs must necessarily be more successful than the haphazard interplay of independent individuals has continuously gained ground until to-day there is hardly a political group anywhere in the world which does not want central direction of most human activities in service of one aim or another.
>
> (Hayek, 1963, Chapter 1, Section 1)

Hayek wanted an alternative, substantial body of propaganda, closely argued, intelligently argued, and also polemical. He wrote to influence British wartime propaganda, but also to influence British and later worldwide informed opinion. He wrote neither a manifesto, nor to urge his views on a great, amorphous, group but like Mill to publicize his view to thinking individuals. He shared with Mill and Mises a concern about the power of the mass, of conforming majority opinion over individual expression, and the way their perceptions were being tampered with. Mises' *The Anti-capitalistic Mentality* (1956) complained of the thoroughness by which "dominion over men's minds" had been achieved, such as in a section provocatively titled The Bigotry of the Literati: "The tremendous machine of 'progressive' propaganda and indoctrination has well succeeded in enforcing its taboos. The intolerant orthodoxy of the self-styled 'unorthodox' schools dominates the scene" (Mises, 1956, Chapter 3, Section 5).

It was not with any relish that Hayek concurred with this and with Mill: "[T]he great majority are rarely capable of thinking independently, that on most questions they accept views which they find ready-made, and that they will be equally content if born or coaxed into one set of beliefs or another" (Hayek, 2007, "Probably it is true"). However, Hayek added, "It certainly does not justify the presumption of any group of people to claim the right to determine what people ought to think or believe" (Hayek, 2007, "Probably it is true"). Marx and Engels might claim the capitalist "bourgeoisie" were doing exactly that. Hayek meanwhile was referring to the proponents of socialism, or state economic control, although as will be seen his strictures, like *On Liberty* and not like *The Communist Manifesto*, were extended to any group that tried to seize control of the engines of propaganda. "So long as dissent is not suppressed", Hayek continued,"there will always be some who will query the ideas ruling their contemporaries and put new ideas to the test of argument and propaganda" (Hayek, 2007, "Probably it is true"). "Propaganda", to use it in the way Hayek's generation often used it, was a legitimate testing ground in an individualist society, which echoes Mill's advocacy of publicity, as opposed to "puffery".

The Road to Serfdom was written between 1940 and 1943, driven by Hayek's concern that the war was being used to propagandize economic collectivism and therefore offered a threat to economic and personal liberty. To Hayek, the failure and threat of collectivism stared the Allies in the face, in the forms of their opponents, and also more—controversially for the time— their Soviet ally. In the case of the Nazis, their socialist predecessors had already helped to weaken public belief in individual liberty.

Germany aside, Hayek's attempt to reawaken the British public to the economic foundations for their liberties, was motivated by concern that as economists were busy with official war work, "public opinion on these problems is to an alarming extent guided by amateurs and cranks, by people who have an ax to grind or a pet panacea to sell" (Hayek, 2007, "If in spite of"). This was the source of the "trickery" Mises had warned of. A communication struggle was underway, in which popular or virtuous words had been co-opted by one side, emptied of their meaning and turned into virtues simply by dint of frequent repetition, supported by pseudo-technical phrases. Mises had complained around fifteen years earlier "of the zealous propaganda of the antiliberal parties, which twists the facts the other way round" (Mises, 1927, Introduction, Section 5). Hayek was careful to imprison misused words between quotation marks: "scientific", "progressive" were being used, as Marx had used them, to create a fallacious, pseudo-scientific idea that a planned society was "inevitable" (perhaps the word Hayek disliked most of all, for what he viewed as its deadening effect on human freedom and stifling impact on debate). While writing *The Road to Serfdom*, Hayek had also developed arguments in "The Counter-revolution of Science" (1941, further developed in 1952) examining the French early socialist and sociologist, the Comte de Saint-Simon (1760–1825), and through his legacy questioning the validity and integrity of applying scientific methods to the social sciences, and ultimately to social policy. Hayek discussed a passage by the influential Saint-Simonian Léon Halévy (1802–83) that underlines the direction his writing was taking in *The Road to Serfdom*:

> He [Halévy] sees the time approaching when the "art of moving the masses" will be so perfectly developed that the painter, the musician, and the poet "will possess the power to please and to move with the same certainty as the mathematician solves a geometrical problem or the chemist analyses any substance. Then only will the moral side of society be firmly established".
>
> (Hayek, 1941, p. 137)

"[T]he art of the modern Ministers of Propaganda would have been fully appreciated and were even foreseen by the Saint-Simonians" Hayek ended (Hayek, 1941, p. 137). To him, statist views were chimeras conjured into reality by the clever direction of public opinion, whereby:

Facts and theories must thus become no less the object of an official doctrine than views about values. And the whole apparatus for spreading knowledge—the schools, and the press, radio and motion picture—will be used exclusively to spread those views.

(Hayek, 2007, "Facts and theories")

He described this cocktail of propaganda, utopianism, the social sciences and misplaced scientific analyses as "scientism", introducing the term in "Scientism and the study of society", which appeared in two parts in 1942 and 1943. The success of the "physical and biological disciplines" and the application of the term "science" to them attracted imitators in other fields unsuited to their methods (Hayek, 1942, p. 268; Hayek, 2007, "This is not the place"). "Thus the tyranny commenced which the methods and technique of the Sciences in the narrow sense of the term have ever since exercised over the other subjects" (Hayek, 1942, p. 268).

In *The Road to Serfdom* he emphasised the consequence of this change: "an entire abandonment of the individualist tradition which has created western civilization" (Hayek, 2007, "All we are here").

Scientism, a deformed, politicized version of scientific enquiry, was changing public opinion by dominating wartime propaganda. Just as Mill had worried about the tendency of popular media to generate conformity of opinion, whether unwittingly or not, Hayek also recognized its power. "To 'plan' or 'organize' the growth of the mind, or, for that matter, progress in general, is a contradiction in terms" (Hayek, 2007, "This interaction of individuals"). It was this part of Hayek's thinking, if not his views on the economy, with which the erstwhile socialist writer George Orwell agreed in his famous short review of *The Road to Serfdom,* written four years before his own assault on the centralized management of mass communication in *1984.* Orwell's review stated:

It cannot be said too often—at any rate, it is not being said nearly often enough—that collectivism is not inherently democratic, but, on the contrary, gives to a tyrannical minority such powers as the Spanish Inquisitors never dreamed of.

(Orwell, 1944)

Orwell did not believe economic liberty led to personal liberty. Hayek, though, wished to restate the case for the economic aspect of personal liberty. Hayek plainly understood the thoroughness with which traditional and non-traditional media platforms could be organized around a single theme, leaving little space for the individual to breathe. It was strongly expressed in the opening paragraphs of Chapter Eleven, The end of truth: "[T]he effect of propaganda in totalitarian countries is different not only in magnitude but in kind from that of the propaganda made for different ends by independent and competing agencies" (Hayek, 2007, "This is, of course").

Today the former might be viewed as propaganda, and the latter as PR, though that was less clear-cut then. The difference accepted by many at the time, and which remains relevant, lay not with the name, but in the view that "what is truly vicious is not propaganda but a monopoly of it", a line credited to many but originating with that fervent and successful propagandist Napoleon Bonaparte (Holtman, 1950, p. i), whose diverse techniques still deserve study (Bernays, 1980; Hanley, 2005; Holtman, 1950; Leith, 1965).

Cautiously accepting for a moment that differences between the two terms "propaganda" and "PR" have now bifurcated enough to have some different characteristics, it may be said that Hayek had studied enough of the former to understand its potential power over the latter. A footnote to the chapter reminded the reader of the Nazis' coordination (*Gleichschaltung*) of all activities to enforce the message of their legitimacy, and thus the "*Gleichschaltung* of all minds" (Hayek, 2007, "This is, of course"). To Hayek, the connection between communication freedom, economic freedom and personal freedom is clear. Like Mill, he wished to defend the human potential for spontaneity, against the idea that: "Every activity must derive its justification from a common social purpose" (Hayek, 2007, "It is entirely in"). *Gleichschaltung*, whether Nazi, Socialist or Communist to him meant: "There must be no spontaneous, unguided activity, because it might produce results which cannot be foreseen and for which the plan does not provide" (Hayek, 2007, "It is entirely in").

According to Hayek, statist cheerleaders believed that coordination of opinion was happening anyway, so "we ought to use this power deliberately to turn the thoughts of the people in what we think is a desirable direction" (Hayek, 2007, "The desire to force"). Hayek says of the first assumption "probably it is true enough". He is dilating on a theme we have seen developing in Marx and Engels, Mill, Carlyle, Lippmann, and others mentioned earlier, including the novelist Edgar Allen Poe (1809–49) in the nineteenth century in his short story "The man of the crowd" (1840) about the craving of isolated people to be part of the urban mass, or Sherwood Anderson's (1876–1941) "Winesburg, Ohio" (1919) eighty years later, recalling a spreading conformity of opinion in rural districts by the 1890s. Hayek sympathized:

> There is no real freedom of thought in our society, so it is said, because the opinions and tastes of the masses are shaped by propaganda, by advertising, by the example of the upper classes, and by other environmental factors which inevitably force the thinking of people into well-worn grooves.
> (Hayek, 2007, "The desire to force")

Nevertheless, he continued—and this is a point reiterated over and again in *The Road to Serfdom*: "It shows a complete confusion of thought to suggest that, because under any sort of system the majority of people follow the lead of somebody, it makes no difference if everybody has to follow the same lead" (Hayek, 2007, "Probably it is true").

Finally, Hayek identified one more outcome of State-monopolized communication. Perhaps it is one of the longest-lasting problems in post-totalitarian states, that of social amorality, or "the spirit of complete cynicism as regards truth which it engenders, the loss of the sense of even the meaning of truth" (Hayek, 2007, "The general intellectual").

Propaganda misuse, then, occupies a large portion of *The Road to Serfdom.* A case could be made for saying that it was as big a concern for Hayek as the future for classical liberalism, for it is possible to see public communication taking its place alongside the book's supposed main thesis, or rather the thesis for which it is best remembered. Many analyses of his book have little to say on the subject. Communication is once again essential but apparently invisible, through no intention of the author. At least one reaction to the book in *The Modern Language Journal,* by Sheila Kragness, then a doctoral student, paid the subject sustained attention: "To what degree such misuse of language is typical of totalitarian ideology is not always fully appreciated. The situation is described in *The Road to Serfdom*" (Kragness, 1945, p. 521).

The problem of the "audience"

Hayek did not neglect target audiences. He knew that propaganda needed them, including his own, but wrestled with the implications for individual liberty. He sought out the individual, feared but did not know how to sidestep the collective "masses" socialism cultivated, and his limited PR knowledge stopped him considering how to connect with alternative groups that were neither so small as the individual nor so big as the "masses".

Seeking the individual

Hayek joins Mill, Luther, Gandhi and Jung in ostensibly directing his message to individuals instead of larger groupings favored by Confucius, Plato, al-Farabi, Clausewitz, Marx and Engels.

"This interaction of individuals, possessing different knowledge and different views, is what constitutes the life of thought" he concluded (Hayek, 2007, "This interaction of"). Yet Hayek felt the existence, however unhelpful, of the enormous public his chosen opponents preferred—the one known, feared, desired, embraced and managed as the "masses". From the nineteenth century we have seen how this group presented thoughtful people with pressing questions. Should it be contained or emancipated? To Marx and Engels of course "Masses of labourers, crowded into the factory" were the inevitable agents of Revolution (Marx and Engels, 1998, p. 43). Oswald Spengler occupied a more nationalist, still socialist but avowedly not national socialist position. In his great work *The Decline of the West,* the German historian feared, with Mill, the susceptibility of the free twentieth-century masses as "in the background, unseen, the new forces are fighting one another by buying the press" (Spengler, 1926, "In the contests of")."Today a democrat of the old school would demand, not freedom for the press, but freedom from the press" (Spengler, 1926, "In preparation for"). Spengler overlooked other publicity techniques, and once again along with the thinkers discussed here largely or entirely neglected developments in the commercial or general non-political arenas. Perhaps because of this missing perspective, he declared that the mass always existed to be led by someone:

> No tamer has his animals more under his power. Unleash the people as reader-mass and it will storm through the streets and hurl itself upon the target indicated, terrifying and breaking windows; a hint to the press-staff and it will become quiet and go home.
>
> (Spengler, 1926, "In the contests of")

Trapped by the "masses"

Hayek reacted against Spengler's prediction of traditional liberalism's "inevitable decay" before "a new age of Caesarism" as strongly as he reacted against Statism (Hayek, 2007, Chapter 12, Editor's footnote 27). Spengler's Caesarism meant a dictator's power exercised through pliant, moribund political institutions. As Hayek was concerned, Caesarism embraced Marxism. He quoted with approval a British writer's declaration that "in all essentials" Marxism "is Fascism and National Socialism" (Hayek, 2007, "Mr Eastman's case"). Hayek's agreement with Mill about the tyranny of the majority nevertheless meant that he could not shake off the idea of the masses as an audience guided by managed public communication. He accepted its current reality and feared it: "such a numerous and strong group with fairly homogeneous views is not likely to be formed by the best but rather by the worst elements of any society" because "if we wish to find a high degree of uniformity and similarity of outlook, we have to descend to the regions of lower moral and intellectual standards where the more primitive and 'common' tastes prevail" (Hayek, 2007, "There are three").

Hayek's comments on the susceptibility of the masses to propaganda and advertising were recorded earlier. He felt the mass was an obstacle to freedom, "barbarous offspring" created by socialists to provide an audience for "the general acceptance of a common Weltanschauung, of a definite set of values" (Hayek, 2007, "Socialists, the cultivated"). Hayek's remarks support Bernay's advice to western democracies to study Communist PR: "It was in these efforts to produce a mass movement supported by such a single world view that the socialists first created most of the instruments of indoctrination of which the Nazis and Fascists have made such effective use" (Hayek, 2007, "Socialists, the cultivated").

The "mass" justified a political party. The first was the socialists, practicing comprehensive, or totalitarian, communication aimed at standardizing perception, opinion and action, a party that "embraces all activities of the individual from the cradle to the grave, which claims to guide his views on everything, and which delights in making all problems questions of party Weltanschauung" (Hayek, 2007, "In Germany and Italy").

Like the other thinkers here, Hayek had to identify his audiences so he or his opponents could mobilize or undermine them, and at present his opponents' perceptions of those audiences were prevailing. Once an audience (or audiences) is identified and accepted, targeted propaganda may accelerate and is more easily coordinated, shown by the use of the masses, "usually the more highly skilled industrial workers" according to Hayek, echoing Marx and Engels' identification of the proletariat: "The movement", Hayek wrote, "is immediately concerned with the status of one particular group, and its aim is to raise that status relatively to other groups" (Hayek, 2007, "So long as the").

Hayek seems to have agreed socialism's audience targeting was too simplistic. Identifying the mass, or proletariat, as one of only two key publics was compromised and out-dated by those individual aspirations described by Le Bon (see Chapter Seven), or by "disregarded" smaller audiences that could not be grouped into the political target created by socialists. They were the "countless army of clerks and typists, administrative workers and schoolteachers, tradesmen and small officials, and the lower ranks of the professions" (Hayek, 2007, "Socialist theory and"). Some of these provided leadership for the socialists, it was true, but the socialist ideology and socialist message was not made for this, or these, groups. In the end though, he could not erase his opponents' perspective and accepted the reality of the spectre they had raised. "If a numerous group is needed, strong enough to impose their views on the values of life on all the rest", he wrote, "it will be those who form the "mass" in the derogatory sense of the term, the least original and independent, who will be able to put the weight of their numbers behind their particular ideals" (Hayek, 2007, "In the first instance").

Overlooking the alternatives

Did Hayek need to accept his opponent's target audiences on their own terms? The invalidity of establishing two enormous audiences and identifying them as friends or foe was laid bare by Bernays when he listed some of America's many alternative identities: the trade associations, non-profits and trade publications, and quoted *Life* Magazine's satirical list of alternative US publics ("the Colonial Dames, the Masons, Kiwanis and Rotarians, the K of C, the Elks" etc.) to a Briton praising America for having no upper or lower class. "It is extremely difficult to realize how many and diverse are the cleavages in our society" he wrote in 1928, referring to commercial, racial, religious, economic and other subdivisions that distracted people from seeing themselves as a politicized "mass" (Bernays, 2005, "It is extremely"). Mises was also more confident about the survival of private property from attack from all sides, including "the resentment of the masses—itself deeply rooted in instinctive envy" (Mises, 1927, Chapter 2, Section 3).

Hayek was constrained by his limited knowledge of "propaganda" and its metamorphosis into private sector "public relations", which would have helped him develop anti-socialist propaganda that utilized Bernays' more accurate classifications. Perhaps he could have circumvented his concern about the masses if he had paid more attention to the private, non-governmental world of associations and communities where most people obstinately tend to live out their lives. He did not, however, and for that reason largely used— and with Mill and Spengler feared—the audience identities used by his politicized opponents, even overlooking the energy of the audience-creating process in a free-market. New prosperity had created new identities alongside surviving older ones: an unanticipated outcome of the continual destruction of the "fixed, frozen" social relations recounted by Marx and Engels, a destructiveness *The Communist Manifesto* applied to everything except its supposedly monolithic target audience.

PR and the fate of the individual

The Road to Serfdom owes its existence to Hayek's ideas about communication in public affairs. He continues the trajectory that began with Luther, in which public intellectuals found themselves facing, more and more, the requirement to engage large numbers of people, to develop messages that helped this process, and to understand some of the techniques used in mass communication. That understanding was incomplete because of an incomplete understanding of the expanding publicity machine. Nineteenth- and twentieth-century thinkers often feared it, rather than applied it as a technical tool—perhaps because it too was a product of the radically destabilizing experiences of industrialization, urbanization and social unrest.

Hayek did not grasp the true extent of the process either, but was less suspicious of propaganda in the round. He disliked the ways some of its most effective practitioners, particularly totalitarian states, turned arts and social sciences into "the most fertile factories of the official myths which the rulers use to guide the minds and wills of their subjects" (Hayek, 2007, "This applies even"). He was concerned about the misuse—or re-purposing—of key words on an industrial scale to shift perception. He presented the case for a solid bedrock of substantive opinion on which to build a case and a future; and the need for that opinion to be technical, grounded in careful argument but not too technical or obscure. He showed awareness that emotion could be misdirected, reasoning manipulated and independent thought drained from a public communication campaign—the antithesis of Gandhi's experience. Nevertheless, Hayek was keen to use publicity techniques to send his own message; which did not seek to push groups into a particular set of State-sanctioned principles, but urged individuals to make free choices about the direction of their economic and therefore social interactions. It was the practical, libertarian expression of

Mill's classical liberal principles in the public arena. PR today sometimes tries to make audience members feel their individuality; much more so than Gandhi, let alone Hayek. On the other hand, it can also send individuals in a particular direction on behalf of their clients, using programs of managed communication that are more comprehensive than ever before in history. Prosaic manufacturers of cosmetics, breakfast cereals, environmental campaigns or medicines must develop messages to guide targeted audiences towards certain opinions about social issues, or particular views about how lives should be experienced, self-esteem felt, and children raised.

These PR activities are not strictly totalitarian since alternative messages exist, but they are totalitarian to the extent of seeking to create, often in vivid detail, a cradle-to-grave view of the world beyond the immediate product. Hayek was right about the power of modern propaganda (or PR) to deliver tsunamis of information around such coordinated themes, but he focussed on the State. Should he have turned his guns on other targets? Unlike Bernays, who was profiting from the process, Hayek did not ask if the same trend was developing elsewhere in society, or whether it too was affecting perceptions about systems of governments and economics. The urgent circumstances in the time he was writing probably stopped him from doing this. Possibly his own economic principles would have stopped him from considering this commercial version of propaganda in any case. Propaganda to him was a political, not corporate, matter.

One achievement of *The Road to Serfdom* is to raise much bigger questions about society's embrace of PR: perhaps the biggest questions of all. Can an individual ever cut ties from PR? What happens to people when organizations fold their individuality into the collective personality of a particular audience? Can even the best-intentioned organizations avoid creating collective identities, and can that collective identity resist PR attempts to manage its perceptions and actions ever more closely? The idea of PR equipped to authentically elide with such a complex organism as the autonomous individual remains out of reach, if it is possible for organizations to reach it in this world at all. Can collectively directed communication engage with the fully realised individual? Jung, whom we shall discuss next, considered this question.

References

Bernays, E. L. (1980) *Public Relations.* Norman: University of Oklahoma Press.
——(2005) *Propaganda.* New York: Ig Publishing.
Fisher, A. G. B. (1944) "Book Review. Hayek, Friedrich von. The Road to Serfdom." *International Affairs* (Royal Institute of International Affairs 1944–), 20(3): 415.
Hanley, W. (2005) *The Genesis of Napoleonic Propaganda, 1796 to 1799.* New York: Columbia University Press.
Hayek, F. A. (1941) "The Counter-revolution of Science." *Economica,* 8(31): 281–320.
——(1942) "Scientism and the Study of Society. Part One." *Economica,* 9(35): 267–91.
——(1943) "Scientism and the Study of Society. Part Two." *Economica,* 10(37): 34–63.

Hayek, F. A. (ed.) (1963) *Collectivist Economic Planning: Critical Studies on the Possibilities of Socialism.* London: Routledge & Kegan Paul. Available at http://mises.org/books/economicplanning.pdf.

Hayek, F. A. (2007) *The Road to Serfdom: Text and Documents.* Edited by B. Caldwell. Chicago, IL: University of Chicago Press.

Holtman, R. B. (1950) *Napoleonic Propaganda.* Baton Rouge: Louisiana State University Press.

Hoselitz, B. F. (1945) "Professor Hayek on German Socialism." *The American Economic Review,* 35(5): 929–34.

Kragness, S. I. (1945) "Critical Thinking through Language." *The Modern Language Journal,* 29(6): 521–23.

Leith, J. A. (1965) *The Idea of Art as Propaganda in France, 1750–1799: A Study in the History of Ideas.* Toronto: University of Toronto Press.

Marx, K. and Engels, F. (1998) *The Communist Manifesto: A Modern Edition.* With an introduction by E. J. Hobsbawm. London: Verso.

Mises. L. von (1985 [1927]) *Liberalism, in the Classical Tradition.* Translated by R. Raico. Edited by A. Goddard with Foreword by L. M. Spadaro and Preface by B. B. Greaves. New York: Foundation for Economic Education.

——(2008 [1956]) *The Anti-capitalistic Mentality.* Auburn, AL: The Ludwig von Mises Institute.

Orwell, G. (1944) "Review of Hayek's *The Road to Serfdom.*" *The Observer,* April 9.

Spengler, O. (1926) *The Decline of the West: Form and Actuality.* Translated by C. F. Atkinson. New York: A. A. Knopf.

11 PR's choice: creating audiences or discovering individuals

Carl Jung (1875–1961), *The Undiscovered Self* (1957)

PR's threat to the psyche

Every work in this book accepts the malleability of human nature as a fact. It has often been viewed as a good thing, or at least as a reality that can be used to promote an idea or cause. Not so in *The Undiscovered Self*, however. The author and psychologist Carl Jung joins Mill in warning that our individuality is endangered. He offers resistance to malleability, but his approach differs from Mill, and possibly maps a different course for PR in future.

Why choose this, out of all Jung's works? Why Jung in particular, out of many well-recorded connections between PR and psychology? Because, it may be replied, of the way the connections are explored in this essay, enriched by an accompanying piece excerpted from his 1950 Collected Works and titled "Symbols and the Interpretation of Dreams" (each essay is briefly denoted in the following references as "Undiscovered" or "Symbols").

The Undiscovered Self is certainly not a practical essay; not an *On War*, *On the Perfect State* or *The Republic*. Not even an *On Liberty* or *Autobiography of My Experiments with Truth*. Not applied at all except as psychology. What it does do is raise problems PR still faces, with its increasingly persuasive tools and more organizations trying to use them. These problems include the relationship between emotions and ideologies, also discussed by Hayek; the case for a spiritual dimension that bridges the public and private spheres of action, demonstrated by Gandhi; the troubled relationship between the masses, public communication and individual autonomy, discussed by Gandhi and Hayek.

The Undiscovered Self has been described as one of the three or four most important of Jung's writings that are concerned with politics (Odajnyk, 1973, p. 142). His concern is limited, and consulting other work, including "Symbols and the Interpretation of Dreams" is necessary to bring out the ideas in this essay. We are also hampered by a lack of synthesis. Jung's autobiographical collaborator Aniela Jaffé reminds us "Jung never felt any disposition to offer a summary of his ideas—either in conversation or in writing". Jung explained "I should have to omit all my evidence and rely on a type of categorical statement which would not make my results any easier to understand" (Jaffé in Jung, 1989, "The chapter entitled"). Furthermore he felt "ultimate definition was not possible. He [Jung] thought it wise to let the inexplicable elements that always cling to psychic realities remain as riddles or mysteries" (Jung, 1989, "The short glossary").

Jung's thinking on public communication developed in his later work when reflecting on politics, religion, public life and individuality prompted other reflections on the role of PR (or "propaganda" as he calls it, like his contemporary Hayek). In doing so, Jung questions many forces that have defined PR's role since the early twentieth century. *The Undiscovered Self* is not about "business", it is not about "PR strategy", but it is about PR, because PR mediates the frontier where organizations meet society, and ethical PR seeks to respect and understand the autonomy of its target audiences. Jung contributes to these subjects because he has affected our view of ourselves, and on preserving our individuality from external forces infiltrating conscious thinking and behaviour. To Mill, Marx and Engels, this happened because industrialization had left individuals susceptible to mass influences, which *On Liberty* and *The Road to Serfdom* feared, not always for the same reasons, and *The Communist Manifesto* managed for a greater good. Gandhi looked to merge individuality and ethics in his campaign communication. Jung was concerned about this question also, as observer rather than participant. An observation from Kafka in 1917 perhaps helps us comprehend Jung's fears: "Human nature, essentially changeable, unstable as the dust, can endure no restraint; if it binds itself it soon begins to tear madly at its bonds, until it rends everything asunder, the wall, the bonds, and its very self" (Kafka, 1971, "The Great Wall of China").

At the end of his life Jung repeated his own fears for human nature, which appeared posthumously in *Memory, Dreams, Reflections* (1963). Man "is fatally handicapped by the weakness of his conscious and the corresponding fear of the unconscious", his "beginnings" "live with him as the constant substratum of his existence, and his consciousness is as much molded by them as by the physical world around him" (Jung, 1989, "The Word happens"). Meanwhile, psychological methods were failing to nurture "the treasured feeling of individuality" and bring the individual consciousness and unconsciousness into harmony (Jung, 1989, "The Word happens")

Other psychological methods were being used by business and the State, to disrupt individuality and generate fealty. Edward Bernays a nephew of Jung's colleague Sigmund Freud made no bones about doing so on behalf of his clients, incorporating the social sciences in general into his techniques, and successfully publicizing the fact. He described the evolution of his ideas in *Public Relations* (1952): "I had been exposed at home to discoveries about the mind and individual and group behavior" (Bernays, 1980, "I was thus"). The possibilities crystallized early in Bernays' career, when he worked with the Creel Committee, established in 1917 (the year of Kafka's aforementioned essay) to "further a better knowledge everywhere of the war aims and ideals of the United States" (Bernays, 1980, "I worked with"). Bernays described it as a "turning point" alerting him to the power of PR, over traditional "press agentry", and also credited his interest in psychology. In *Public Relations* he recommended his uncle's lectures on psychoanalysis: "Consistent study of these findings and others, as they are published, is now imperative for the advertising man" (Bernays, 1980, "Our total behavior").

Five years after *Public Relations,* Jung published *The Undiscovered Self,* which suggested a very different relationship between psychoanalysis and PR. In *Modern Man in Search of a Soul* (1933) Jung had agreed with Freud that terrible stresses were being placed on modern men and women: in the psyche, between the material and non-material, the luminous and shadowed (feelings unregistered by the conscious). All these problems were manifest in the widening gap between our conscious and unconscious selves—since "almost the half of our lives is passed in a more or less unconscious state" (Jung, 2011, "The view that dreams"). The mind "has become a dump for moral refuse and a source of fear" (Jung, 1990, Symbols, p. 606), wrote Jung, though famously he felt Freud's focus on sexual libido did not tell the whole story. For Jung, the psyche and psychological disturbance signalled an ancient craving for spiritual nourishment, through contact with its symbols.

These needs were threatened by several modern developments, including the practice of psychology itself which over-emphasised collective standards and conscious contents over individuality and irrationalism (Jung, 1990, Undiscovered, p. 562). Questions are inevitably raised about managed public communication in conscious society, its chosen targets and the words and symbols it deployed. Jung took the same position as Mill and Hayek, which was a political rather than commercial perspective, arguing in the same piece that: "in so far as society is itself composed of de-individualized human beings, it is completely at the mercy of ruthless individualists" (Jung, 1990, Undiscovered, p. 535), destroying reflection and opening the way to authoritarianism. (Jung, 1990, Undiscovered, p. 489).

More specifically, the "onslaught from outside" was changing the psychologist–patient relationship:

> The psychic situation of the individual is so menaced nowadays by advertising, propaganda, and other more or less well-meant advice and suggestions that for once in his life the patient might be offered a relationship that does not repeat the nauseating "you should," "you must" and similar confessions of impotence.
>
> (Jung, 1990, Undiscovered, p. 534)

The conscious remedy of mass action, described in Gandhi's *Autobiography* and in *The Communist Manifesto,* is for Jung part of the unconscious problem: "A million zeros joined together do not, unfortunately, add up to one. Ultimately everything depends on the quality of the individual, but our fatally shortsighted age thinks only in terms of large numbers and mass organizations" (Jung, 1990, Undiscovered, p. 535).

The Undiscovered Self is counsel to psychologists looking to salvage their patient's self from the danger of the mass, wherein "the individual becomes morally and spiritually inferior" (Jung, 1990, Undiscovered, p. 536). As part of this recovery Jung seeks to understand the impact of "propaganda" on the individual as an individual, and as a member of a larger audience—but not necessarily the monolithic "mass" feared by Mill and Hayek, and harnessed by Clausewitz or Marx and Engels. Jung seems to suggest that creating an audience can be dangerous, whatever form it takes: "Let it [society] band together into groups and organizations as much as it likes—it is this banding together and the resultant extinction of the individual personality that makes it succumb so readily to a dictator" (Jung, 1990, Undiscovered, p. 535).

Unless individuality is recovered from the barrage of communication that subsumes it into political, religious or other groupings, we are left with "the congenital vice of our age: the supremacy of the word ... The word has literally become our god and so it has remained, even if we know of Christianity only from hearsay. Words like 'Society' and 'State' are so concretized that they are almost personified" (Jung, 1990, Undiscovered, p. 554).

One of his collaborators wrote: "Jung explicitly declared his allegiance to history" (Jaffé in Jung, 1989, "Jung explicitly declared"), having discovered that "the psyche spontaneously produces images with a religious content, that it is "by nature religious" (Jung, 1989, "Jung was led"). The agencies best positioned to rescue individuality are therefore churches, but they subscribed to the temptation to view people as communities, or groups and not as people. "They do not bother themselves overmuch with their real task of helping the individual to achieve a *metanoia*, a rebirth of the spirit" (Jung, 1990, Undiscovered, p. 536). Accordingly, rebirth became one of the tasks Jung took on himself, still believing religion was best equipped to act to "counterbalance to mass mindedness", "maintain the psychic balance" and check "definite collective belief" (Jung, 1990, Chapter 2); better equipped than he, and certainly better equipped than the State, which "grants the individual a right to exist only in so far as he is a function of the State" (Jung, 1990, Undiscovered, p. 510).

Another threat to the individual psyche with implications for public communication was the perversion of human emotion by crushing out irrationality in conscious life, the irrationality that linked conscious to unconscious. "Through scientific understanding, our world has become dehumanized" (Jung, 1990, Symbols, p. 585). This was not a rejection of all scientific inquiry, but a comment on one of its by-products, that damage was inevitably being done to "the real inner world of man" when "at least the surface of our world seems to be purified of all superstitious and irrational admixtures" (Jung, 1990, Symbols, p. 587). Jung also had views on the way the last scraps of the irrational and emotional in public life were being distorted by communication. As will be shown, scientific conformity represented an "enormous loss" which was "compensated by the symbols in our dreams" (Jung, 1990, Symbols, p. 585), but for reasons of "mental equilibrium and physiological health" it was "much better for the conscious and unconscious to be connected and to move on parallel lines than for them to be dissociated" (Jung, 1990, Symbols, p. 475).

Jung's path to reviving the individual did not involve economics (although it presumably would have equated at least somewhat with Hayek's individualist approach), or ethical collective action (presumably because he believed it hard to find an ethical leader capable of protecting individuality). He recoiled from the spirit of the age, as leading thinkers are wont to do, with its overreliance on rationalism, and the reduction of philosophy to "an exclusively intellectual and academic exercise" (Jung, 1990, Undiscovered, p. 550). Disruptions to the psychic balance of the individual created an "unendurable rift" between our inner and outer worlds that "cannot simply be replaced by a new rational configuration" (Jung, 1990, Undiscovered, p. 549).

The Word

One of the main contributors to this state of affairs was a propaganda by-product—the power of certain words over others, and the kind of organizations controlling them. The weight of mass communication was rationalist, material and served a flawed Weltanschauung centred on promoting collective identity, on groups rather than individuals, on materiality not spirituality and on a State-directed society. Much now depended on the equilibrium of society's leaders. A crisis was being created that threatened "blood, fire and radioactivity" (Jung, 1990, Undiscovered, p. 561).

When access to the Divine is severed, something called "Society is elevated to the rank of a supreme ethical principle" to be directed by the State, "the inexhaustible giver of all good" and:

> belief in the word becomes credulity, and the word itself … capable of any deception. … With credulity come propaganda and advertising to dupe the citizen with political jobbery and compromises, and the lie reaches proportions never known before in the history of the world.
>
> (Jung, 1990, Undiscovered, p. 554)

To Jung and his followers, anything that takes our evolving individuality and plunges it back into a managed collective from whence it came is necessarily harmful. In Jung's *Man and his Symbols* (1964) a posthumously published work, the Swiss psychologist Marie-Louise von Franz discusses the threat to the "secret activities of the unconscious". "Through these unconscious ties those who belong together come together. That is one reason why attempts to influence people by advertisements and political propaganda are destructive, even when inspired by idealistic motives" (Jung and Franz, 1968, "All activities and").

Jung is perhaps most popularly known for his work on the psychological meaning of symbols in our dreams and waking hours, collective representations tapping the dawn of human consciousness, but words also interested him, in particular the symbolism of the archetypal "Word". Jung's Word was the Christian *Logos*, the Word of God, numinous and mysterious, resonating in our unconscious because it "always belongs to the economy of a living individual" (Jung, 1990, Symbols, p. 589).

However, new "Words" were being made by the twentieth-century State, offering secular archetypes or idealizations for humanity to reverence. This development, assisted by managed public communication, caused Jung to argue in the same piece that: "We have stripped all things of their mystery and numinosity" (Jung, 1990, Symbols, p. 582). The Word "has in our day become a source of suspicion and distrust of all against all" (Jung, 1990, Undiscovered, p. 555), converting it to "an infernal slogan capable of any deception" (Jung, 1990, Undiscovered, p. 554).

"Through one-sidedness the psyche disintegrates and loses its capacity for cognition" (Jung, 1989, "The psyche cannot"), and the disconnection between the word and the divine makes organizations personified and divine, as they use the word's power (and the power of symbols) for their own purposes, separating citizens from their foundations (Jung, 1990, Undiscovered, p. 557).

Individuals constantly face altered conditions of existence and the need to adapt, and the combination of their "learning capacity" and the "progressive alienation" already described created a major source of "psychic disturbances and difficulties" (Jung, 1990, Undiscovered, p. 557).

Target audiences for hollow words

"The suffocating power of the masses is paraded before our eyes in one form or another every day in the newspapers" (Jung, 1990, Undiscovered, p. 539). Jung's remark is reminiscent of Mill, except Mill was concerned with public policy and Jung with the inner essence of our individuality, although we have seen Mill touch on this when he hoped individual eccentricities would be respected and encouraged in society and particularly by the press. In Jung's view, this hope was not being realized. The newspapers and propaganda generally per-petuated hollow words by doing what publicity must do to earn its living. Words emptied of true (and filled with false) spiritual content could not con-nect individual consciousness to its unconscious shadow. Instead, they treated individuals as members of new or existing groups which served an organiza-tion's purpose, especially the "dictator State and denominational religion" (Jung, 1990, Undiscovered, p. 516).

One problematic word, idea and audience was "community", which has much PR currency today. Jung viewed its use in public life with scepticism. Under Communism and religion the word had decoupled from the natural individual need for community ties (Jung, 1990, Undiscovered, p. 511) and "is thrust down the throats of the people so much that is has the exact opposite of the desired effect: it inspires divisive mistrust" (Jung, 1990, Undiscovered, p. 516). This was written in the wake of the failed Hungarian uprising, which may also have influenced Jung's observation that: "The communal ideal reckons without its host, overlooking the individual human being, who in the end will assert his claims" (Jung, 1990, Undiscovered, p. 516).

In general, the "dictator State" (it is unclear here if Jung means all states or Communist states) and religion (again no mention of business): "lay quite particular emphasis on the idea of community" (Jung, 1990, Undiscovered, p. 516), "robbing the individual of his rights" by "depriving him of the metaphysical foundations of his existence" (Jung, 1990, Undiscovered, p. 515). "Community"—or the way it was used—"is an indispensable aid in the organization of masses" because "the hope of or belief in a 'communal experience' makes up for the painful lack of cohesion" (Jung, 1990, Undiscovered, p. 516).

This remark was also directed at churches. Jung believed the individual and the group must co-exist, but felt an imbalance that stifled spiritual self-transformation, caused by the universal consequences of a massive propaganda-directed lurch toward the communal. Jung today might be considering the part large corporations played in this situation, increasing the numbers "of a collectively excited group ruled by affective judgments and wish-fantasies" (Jung, 1990, Undiscovered, p. 490).

Jung's connected point that the "bigger the crowd the more negligible the individual becomes" (Jung, 1990, Undiscovered, p. 503) was reemphasized in his part-written, part-recorded and edited *Memories, Dreams, Reflections* where he remembered that "Between 1918 and 1920, I began to understand that the goal of psychic development is the self" (Jung, 1989, "During those years"). That "path to the center" was achieved by individuation, or inner transformation that let an individual "differentiate himself from all the others and stand on his own feet. All collective identities, such as membership in organizations, support of 'isms,' and so on, interfere with the fulfillment of this task" (Jung, 1989, "The secret society"), because they can manage and constrain individuality, create "mass-mindedness and obstruct its personal, unique engagement with the unconscious by *metanoia* or spiritual rebirth via the "inner images" of dreams. Jung described the impact of his insight: "I hit upon this stream of lava, and the heat of its fires reshaped my life" (Jung, 1989, "It has taken me"). The outer world was not allowing this process to occur, and that is what brought Jung into contact with the role played by managed public communication around group identities. At the end of his life he paid close attention to the part played by the collective: "Psychotherapy has hitherto taken this matter far too little into account" (Jung, 1989, "A collective problem"). Jung's most detailed insight on this appears in *Memories, Dreams, Reflections,* and is quoted here in full:

A collective problem, if not recognized as such, always appears as a personal problem, and in individual cases may give the impression that something is out of order in the realm of the personal psyche. The personal sphere is indeed disturbed, but such disturbances need not be primary;

they may well be secondary, the consequence of an insupportable change in the social atmosphere. The cause of the disturbance is, therefore, not to be sought in the personal surroundings, but rather in the collective situation.

(Jung, 1989, "A collective problem")

If PR helps to thrust aside an individual "in favour of anonymous units that pile up into mass formations" (Jung, 1990, Undiscovered, p. 499); or in coaxing individuals to commit their identity to an audience, whether commercial, racial, political or any other, then PR practitioners must—if Jung is right—recognize that engaging, interacting and conversing with people as audiences, for whatever motive, might do damage to individual autonomy. Whether this is a bad thing may be among PR's main questions, but whether it is happening or not is the first question. Jung's reflections on the collective are, then, a compelling starting point for considering PR's effect on society. An observation from Franz in *Man and his Symbols* may be added:

Attempts to influence public opinion by means of newspapers, radio, television and advertising are based on two factors. On the one hand, they rely on sampling techniques that reveal the trend of "opinion" or "wants"—that is, of collective attitudes. On the other, they express the prejudices, projections and unconscious complexes (mainly the power complex) of those who manipulate public opinion.

(Jung and Franz, 1968, "Attempts to influence")

Propaganda possesses the means to cultivate the collective psyche, undermine the individual until "what alone matters is the blind movement of the masses" (Jung, 1990, Undiscovered, p. 515). Jung described the "'magical' action" of "brass bands, flags, banners, parades, and monster demonstrations" (Jung, 1990, Undiscovered, p. 513). Machiavelli did the same in *The Prince* (1513) with the difference that Machiavelli uses them as tools for legitimizing power, and Jung criticizes them as tools for encouraging collective feelings of security with the State as its "supreme principle": "magic has above all a psychological effect whose importance should not be underestimated" (Jung, 1990, Undiscovered, p. 512).

The individual psyche, with its inbuilt thirst for individuation, suffers damage but is too resilient to produce permanent success for collective propaganda: "All mass movements, as one might expect, slip with the greatest ease down an inclined plane made up of large numbers" (Jung, 1990, Undiscovered, p. 537). Yet the inner self, though overlooked, cannot change its nature. Man's outward life in a movement "cannot give him as a gift something which he can win for himself only with effort and suffering" (Jung, 1990, Undiscovered, p. 537). Franz, mirroring Jung's view about the long-term ineffectiveness of Communist propaganda, decided that: "No

deliberate attempts to influence the unconscious have yet produced any significant results, and it seems that the mass unconscious preserves its
autonomy just as much as the individual unconscious" (Jung & Franz, 1968,
"If a man").

It seems certain that for now our efforts to collectivize the individual will
not desist, and will intensify as organizations feel they can and must demand
more commitment in more areas of activity and belief from audiences they
have identified. In this situation, "the individual combines with the mass and
thus renders himself obsolete" (Jung, 1990, Undiscovered, p. 501); "putting
the finishing touch to his social depotentiation" (Jung, 1990, Undiscovered,
p. 512) by defining individual life as the pursuit of material objectives set by
social or economic policy (Jung, 1990, Undiscovered, p. 499).

Within this context lay the danger of seeing humanity's problems solely as
problems of the conscious world, leading to "a mass movement purporting to
be the champion of the suppressed". If success is achieved, the movement
creates problems in which "political and social conditions arise which bring
the same ills back again in altered form" because "the root of the evil [the
individual's unconscious] is untouched" (Jung, 1990, Undiscovered, p. 558).
Jung drew these conclusions witnessing the Nazi and Communist regimes in
Europe, and the disturbing impact of mass propaganda, with words and
symbols stripped of their instinctive inner meanings and personified into a
leader or movement.

The PR objective: credulous audiences

"Credulity is one of our worst enemies" (Jung, 1990, Undiscovered, p. 555). It
is a natural trait, and it has appeared elsewhere in this book, to put sins of
society down to credulousness, but with Jung it is the third point in the triangle
whose other two points are the misused Word and mass propaganda.

Credulity is the goal of the State, and totalitarian states more than others:

> Anyone who has once learned to submit absolutely to a collective belief
> and to renounce his eternal right to freedom and the equally eternal duty
> of individual responsibility will persist in this attitude, and will be able to
> march with the same credulity and the same lack of criticism in the
> opposite direction.
>
> (Jung, 1990, Undiscovered, p. 523)

Jung sought a society where credulousness was tamed, the spiritual, unconscious dimensions of the Word were restored, the inner life of the individual
respected and encouraged. In such a world "the value of a community
depends on the spiritual and moral stature of the individuals composing it"
(Jung, 1990, Undiscovered, p. 516). Ludwig von Mises averred: "It will
require many long years of self-education until the subject can turn himself
into the citizen" (Mises, 1985, "The propensity of"). Neither Hayek nor Jung

would have disagreed with that, although Jung might have altered the last five words to read "individuate himself into the individual".

To achieve this, a new relationship with the Word was needed. A new relationship with the Word required a new approach to propaganda, with its tendency to view people in groups or masses for the State or misled denominational creeds to direct. With propaganda and the creation of malleable collective audiences came the power to direct words that count wherever it was willed. This could not happen without knowledge of psychology. It is a problem for Jung, as it was with Hayek, that he did not consider the contribution of business to this process, except for the possibly commonplace comment that "the meaning of life is not exhaustively explained by your business activities, nor is the deep desire of the human heart answered by your bank account" (Jung, 1990, Symbols, p. 604).

We have seen he showed less doubt about the damage done by states: "The Communist revolution had debased man far lower than democratic collective psychology has done" (Jung, 1990, Undiscovered, p. 559). States claimed his attention when he contemplated propaganda, and Jung scholars perpetuate this perspective. As recently as 2001, when private sector PR was advancing into the digital age, *Jung: A Very Short Introduction* at least placed PR experts in a list of occupations dominated by "Extraverted feeling types" (Stevens, 2001, "Extraverted feeling types") but could still only discuss public communication's wide-and-deep-reaching activities by relating it to Hitler's "skilful use of propaganda" against the Jews (Stevens, 2001, "Shadow projection can").

Odajnyk posits that the "post-Enlightenment secular and organizational orientation" mean that "mass psychoses usually appear as political movements" (Odajnyk, 1973, p. 67), but overlooking private sector PR is surely a serious omission in Jungian study. By the time of *The Undiscovered Self* the capacity of business to connect with audiences was comparable to the State's. The Word also lay in the hands of corporations, brands and products, in some cases more than governments. Jung had instead concentrated on the Cold War psyche, the psychological tyranny exerted by Communism and its inherent fragility, despite oppressive propaganda, as shown by the 1956 uprising in Hungary.

Jung did not wish humans to throw themselves into the hubbub of public debate, like Mill; or meld with the collective in a public campaign with strong spiritual dimensions like Gandhi, let alone offer recommendations for the wholesale restructuring of society by mass communication, like Marx, Engels, and most of the earliest works explored here. Jung wished the individual to "serve as his own group, consisting of a variety of opinions and tendencies— which need not necessarily be marching in the same direction" (Jung, 1989, "Nevertheless it may"). Bernays in 1928 applied principles of mass psychology, and "direct observation of the group mind", saying: "The modern propagandist studies systematically and objectively the material with which he is working in the spirit of the laboratory" (Bernays, 2005, "The modern propagandist"). Jung advocated a much more personal awakening, a different relationship with the group, religion and the State, by opening areas of inquiry where traditional scientific methods could not trespass without degenerating into the "scientism" criticized by Hayek.

Jung wrote (and the italics are his): "*Resistance to the organized mass can be effected only by the man who is as well organized in his individuality as the mass itself*" (Jung, 1990, Undiscovered, p. 540). He encouraged the individual not to look for an "undivided goal", but to accept the "jostling together" of the psyche's components, and "a certain degree of dissociation" (Jung, 1990, Undiscovered, p. 540). In Jung's later views about communication, not formulated in detail during his life, there are surely possibilities for making a stronger, deeper, richer, healthier relationship between PR and the individuals composing audiences which today can be more fragmented and fluid, thanks to new media at our disposal.

References

Bernays, E. L. (1980) *Public Relations.* Norman: University of Oklahoma Press.
——(2005) *Propaganda.* New York: Ig Publishing.
Jung, C. G. (1989). *Memories, Dreams, Reflections.* Recorded and edited by A. Jaffé. New York: Vintage Books.
——(1990) *The Undiscovered Self: With Symbols and the Interpretation of Dreams.* Princeton, NJ: Princeton University Press.
——(2011) *Modern Man in Search of a Soul.* Princeton, NJ: Princeton University Press.
Jung, C. G. and Franz, M.-L. (eds) (1968) *Man and his Symbols.* New York: Dell Publishing.
Kafka, F. (1971) "The Great Wall of China." In N. N. Glatzer (ed.) *The Complete Stories.* New York: Schocken Books.
Mises, L. von (1985) *Liberalism: In the Classical Tradition.* Preface by B. B. Greaves. Foreword by L. M. Spadaro. Translated by R. Raico. New York: Foundation for Economic Education.
Odajnyk, W. (1973) "The Political Ideas of C G Jung." *The American Political Science Review,* 67(1): 142–52.
Stevens, A. (2001) *Jung: A Very Short Introduction.* Oxford: Oxford University Press.

12 The future of PR

Irrational or rational? Magical or scientific? Individual or collective?

"In my beginning is my end" said T. S. Eliot, and the end is a useful place to remind us of the point made at the beginning. Communication is the communal act of explaining, learning, and perception sharing, and the works here were made to share a view about society, to explain how that society was to be achieved, to sustain its legitimacy and survive its errors. It is hardly surprising, indeed it is inevitable, that managed public communication features in every case.

Could Confucius have advocated a virtuous state without seeing the need to manage ceremonies, songs, dress, rites and public poetry? Was Plato's Republic viable without a noble lie to feature at all publicly managed occasions? Did a source of PR's future power originate in Luther's volatile brew of passions, terse, pungent language, reason, appeals to the individual soul and public communication? Could Clausewitz have shaped the policies and propaganda of State, military, and the organizations supporting them without grasping the importance of managing willpower?

From the late nineteenth century managed communication attracted closer attention. Marx and Engels identified or imagined two vast audiences and pitted them in communication battle against each other. Mill was concerned for the future of individuality in an age of mass communication, and advocated a State where publicity and individuality could co-exist. Gandhi created a synthesis of individual and collective, using public campaigns and publicity. Hayek understood the techniques used to influence mass opinion, and looked to redirect them against collectivism, by changing their content. Jung more than all the others worried that such communication, as it became more systematic and extensive, not only influenced public policy and political freedom but damaged what it meant to be human.

Only al-Farabi, writing in the tenth century, sought a perfected society without much of the racket that accompanies managed public communication, describing a place free of such distractions, which in that sense at least may be the society dreamed of but not detailed in *The Communist Manifesto*. What is left, unfortunately, is communication directed from one source, which guards the Perfection and cannot be contradicted, a version of Albert Camus' observation about "the gospel preached by totalitarian regimes in the form of a monologue dictated from a lonely mountain" (Camus, 1956, "There is, in fact"). Maybe the noise, heat and dust of competing PR is the best society can do at this moment, to show it is free—presumably so long as competition is protected, and individuality encouraged whatever media and biochemical advances arise to restrain either or both.

Because these ideas have had such a fundamental affect on the societies humans have tried to build, they have directly or (no less powerfully) indirectly, affected the function now called PR. They have affected the media that has been chosen and managed, the audiences that must be worked with, the balance between the appeals to collective and individual sentiment, the intensity of control exercised over dissent, the tone and content of messages. I do not deny for a moment that other thinkers were equally or almost as influential. PR must examine them to better know itself, and what it is capable of.

The works, I think, also reveal shifts in our views about society that then affected our views about PR. We have seen that two factors count in the public arena where these thinkers operated: the idea itself and the effectiveness of its communication. Initially, the idea was that nearly all individuals were inherently unfit to lead in a sophisticated polity and needed organization and guidance to be content. Luther heralded a violent break with that view of the world: now the individual must wrestle with conscience, temptation and fortune and use communication more personally and more aggressively. The age of reason, the enlightenment and most of all Romanticism and revolution loosed the civic potential of the individual personality, while States struggled to collectivize that energy and channel it for their own purposes. As that unfolded, private organizations both commercial and non-profit learned the techniques for themselves and brought them to new levels of creativity and intensiveness. Thinkers, perhaps too engrossed with the government's part in this development, began looking for spaces where individuality could be reclaimed. This tension between the individual and the collective is still evolving in PR strategy; and the emphasis on the collective has not yet been dislodged from its dominant position in spite of the Information Age's new tools. Yet the desire for individual connection, the persistent feeling that individuality means authenticity, must eventually, surely, lead to a fundamentally changed relationship between organizations and people, with PR as a more creative, maybe much less scientific (or "scientistic") mediator. Few if any of the later works had much time for what they saw as an over-application of scientific method in arousing the feelings of their chosen audiences. Many are famous because they spoke of humanity's spiritual, emotional qualities: drawing our autonomy, insight and their reasoning power from those sources. We are not yet free of the Romantic era's sources of inspiration.

It is necessary to acknowledge the fear many of these works showed toward managed public communication. This was a considerable reason behind their view of its power, a power that had either to be censored and supervised, directed unconditionally toward the ultimate vision or objective, or placed in the hands of individuals who were intellectually equipped to use it properly. These concerns are visible in *The Republic's* recommendations for managing key messages and media, and Hayek's fear of individual susceptibility to comprehensive propaganda for State intervention.

Are the later works right to worry about the "scientific" management of public communication and its effect on individuality? As far as PR is concerned, the question begs other familiar questions: do PR's techniques make people freer or more powerless, prosperous or poorer? Does PR leave people better informed, or diverted and distracted from the truth, or over-informed to the point of surrendering their capacity for decision making to others? Are any differences between the modern view of "PR" (managing information in a competitive environment) and "propaganda" (managing information in a monopoly environment) no more than occasional differences of technique or content? Do these works have anything to say on those questions?

Without doubt PR's origins lie in a monopoly environment for communication, and it took thousands of years to move to a competitive environment. Both settings caused concern to many of the thinkers, on the grounds that one or the other could stop society or individuals from achieving a goal: harmony, or virtue, or perfection, emancipation, liberty or self-knowledge. The remedies in these works either involve a benign monopoly of managed communication, or prepare the individual to operate with greater integrity, education or psychological autonomy in monopoly or competitive communication settings.

Nor is there any question that the techniques are interchangeable. The *Russia Today* news service is ostensibly built in the manner of any other global service but has also been called an "ambitious attempt to create a new post-Soviet global propaganda empire" (Harding, 2009). Hannah Arendt wrote in *The Origins of Totalitarianism* (1951) that Nazis "learned from American business publicity" although she felt this similarity was overdrawn: "Businessmen usually do not pose as prophets and they do not constantly demonstrate the correctness of their predictions" (Arendt, 1973, "Propaganda is indeed").

Arendt speaks truly, yet her interpretation is incomplete, and characteristic of that tendency among non-specialists to see public communication in political terms, expressed in multimedia activities directed for or against a State or society. "Propaganda" became pejorative, and associated with State communication monopoly, and the rest has become publicity, or PR. Only not completely, because even in democracies we commonly hear phrases like "Party political propaganda" or "Corporate propaganda", suggesting that public communication is "propaganda" when we disagree with it. Our habit of ignoring definitive definitions causes PR's meaning to slip further through our fingers. Perhaps the most realistic view is Kevin Moloney's description of PR as "weak propaganda" (Moloney, 2006, p. 13) although even that distinction might have baffled many of our surveyed thinkers.

The term "public relations" has hardly escaped criticism, although it was originally encouraged by Bernays as an alternative to "propaganda", which was falling into disrepute. As this book was going to print, a new publication proposed that any reluctance to believe in "public relations" as a discipline was because "it fails to demonstrate adequately the coupling of 'truth' with courage and wisdom" (Demetrious, 2013, p. 3). Kristin Demetrious suggests "public communication" better fits the propagation of those virtues by certain non-profits. Cases and criteria are presented to separate the new phrase from the technocratic, unsavory and corporate inclinations of "PR," and forge an ethical alternative fit for homo *sapiens*, instead of homo *habilis*.

There is something to this. It echoes Gandhi's description of his own activities as "public work" (though he was also comfortable with "propaganda") with its infusion of community and inner spirituality, and claim to virtue. Yet renaming has problems. I suggested in Chapter 1 that a name is often an unhelpful distraction. It is also vulnerable: if one group's choice becomes successful, which is to say "good" or "authentic", it will be co-opted by other groups. It happened to propaganda, public relations, Marxism, and (to Hayek's despair) Liberalism. There is no reason to think it will not continue to happen, however passionately the outraged originators guard a chosen identity. All meanings are compromised by time. It is worth remembering that Confucius, Plato, al-Farabi, Luther and (almost) Clausewitz had no names for this activity, let alone a common one. Despite that, they shared a common activity, and one at least as important to them as to us. Name or no name, it is certain that the tools and principles driving what is currently called PR will continue evolving and subdividing, and that practitioners everywhere will borrow from and build on each other's work.

It would be foolish to ignore the implications for PR in the works we have explored, because all managed public communication shares a scaffolding defined by audience identification, message preparation, setting objectives, overall strategy, specific tactics for delivery and time line. Within this structure, whether it is called propaganda or PR, steps are taken to modify human behaviour. All the works here considered this scaffolding, and the PR profession and also scholarship in general must consider their conclusions. It is under that common framework that powerful and creative persuasiveness emerges to engage society. A more sophisticated understanding of that process is as essential for us as it was for the ten people who featured in this book.

Does PR make us freer and better equipped to "get involved" as constantly urged, or slaves of perceptions enforced either by all the PR special effects a source can wield, or by the numbers of people who accept that source's viewpoint? It does not much matter if we are invited to believe in or endorse a product, cause or policy. The point cannot be the subject itself, and even the kind of PR, or propaganda, is irrelevant in comparison to the choice it presents to us. When we choose based on what has been communicated, are we making it freely or have we been led in a certain direction by the content and "look" of the information, or by our desire to belong or believe in one source over another? We may carry this conundrum further: when we join in this process, standing under PR's "walls of sound" (Moore, 1996, p. 4), are we surrendering our ability to think things out in our own way and ceding it to the perspectives of organizations? It is time we as individuals—not as audiences—examined our "invisible government, which is the true ruling power of our country" (Bernays, 2005, "In theory, every"), wherever our country is. Discounting Bernays' ability to turn a phrase and talent for self-publicity, there is something challenging and worrying in this remark. The techniques now at PR's disposal make the need for this examination, I believe, very pressing indeed.

Individuals must be more "PR literate". We need a deeper understanding of its methods and the role it plays. This might involve learning (and for some relearning) how to distinguish media from message (itself a fraction of the PR literacy we require: understanding the sheer multiplicity of active organizations, their creative approaches and an overall strategic comprehension is more valuable). It might also involve learning not to view one kind of PR as informational and condemn another as propagandist simply because we like or dislike the organizations responsible. A little learning need not promote fear and loathing of the practice itself. It may even help people not to dismiss it, for PR is not insignificant; it is very significant indeed. Through our thinkers we can trace its lengthening reach into the lives of the city, nation, countryside, families, rulers and commoners, into music and poetry, literature, science, politics and religion, commerce and conscience, into war and peace, into the essence of our spirituality and individuality. It cannot be un-invented, even in a utopia. It is interesting that the word "utopia" was created by Sir Thomas More from the Greek for "no place", or "nowhere", but there is no place that PR cannot exist. Another related Classical Greek word, however, means "good place" and any place denying or even controlling public communication cannot easily fall into that category.

The thinkers here were in no doubt about the importance of the topic. They did not pretend it was a sideshow to be dismissed in a few sentences. Serious thought was given to the problems and opportunities raised by managed public communication, and its inescapable impact on society and the individual.

We have also seen how practical they were. Confucius and Plato proposed ways of projecting the right messages with State-managed media. Al-Farabi funnelled non-contradictable, perfected communication through a perfect leader or nearly perfect group of leaders. Even in his World its perfection must be collectively perceived, to deter Earthly chaos and to inch us closer to Divine Truth. Luther disrupted such organization-centered communication, making media everyone's opportunity. Clausewitz urged the warring State to cultivate war-making will among its citizens. Marx and Engels gave guidance for propaganda warfare in the collective struggle against the bourgeois and in particular recognized the importance of audience targeting. Mill recognized publicity and puffing as a central problem of individual liberty, and much of *On Liberty* is about coping with these activities. Gandhi offered detailed and spiritual advice about running issues PR campaigns. Hayek tried to build a propaganda alternative to Statist propaganda. Jung described its threat to the individual. His work on the Word and on collectivized target audiences appears throughout his later writing. None of these writers behaved as if the subject did not exist, none were so naïve as to abolish it from society and their minds. There is no ambivalence among them about its reality. All, including Jung, might have agreed with Bernays' provocative opening to *Propaganda* (deleting in some cases the second last word): "The conscious and intelligent manipulation of the organized habits and opinions of the masses is an important element in democratic society" (Bernays, 2005, "The conscious and").

Is that activity good or bad? Again, these works seems to treat it as inevitable, and because it is inevitable, it must be carefully handled. It could be dangerous, or it could be useful. At the very least its importance should be realized.

What did they fear from misplaced public communication? One group of thinkers feared chaos, moral collapse and the collapse of the State, which alone protected the individual from himself. Another group feared control and subjugation of groups or individuals. For the first group public communication must be controlled to prevent collapse; people must only hear the right music and poetry, attend to the right rituals, receive knowledge only from the lips of the right people who would ideally manage every other form of media. This group includes Confucius, Plato, al-Farabi, Clausewitz (as far as military affairs were involved), Marx and Engels. For the remaining group, the right to use publicity was a civic responsibility, as was the duty to use it properly—and "properly" meant politically, economically, personally, piously, questioningly, ethically. Commercial usage of this potent tool did not particularly interest them, although deeper exploration of corporate communication strategies may have led them to slightly different conclusions and in the case of our last thinker, Jung, this was arguably happening. Only Marx and Engels offered insights into the contribution this process made to capitalism, and its creative, destructive, compulsive tendencies.

From Marx and Engels on, we see concern as public communication grew in volume, in quantity and in the media platforms it used. We find alarm at the fate of the individual—the fate of his or her economic and political liberties, or his or her spiritual, psychological wellbeing. The idea of subordinating a mind to whatever passed as collectively important in the media is unattractive to Mill, Hayek and Jung in particular, as it was to Luther on a single issue. This alarm is related to the deployment of a cod-scientific method to package information, manage audiences, and justify positions, and of course insecure academic disciplines viewed as "soft skills" often succumb to the same temptation. As far as PR is concerned, Hayek rages at fraudulent manipulation of data, Jung at its deadening impact on the psyche. Gandhi preferred a different approach altogether, even as Bernays developed his career by building PR's credibility on "scientific" claims, especially drawn from psychology. Clausewitz, witness of Romanticism and revolution, with his emphasis on willpower and emotion, and his criticism of an overly technical approach to his own discipline, nevertheless shows signs that he may have sympathized with such a view.

In this way, the problem of managed public communication—not the right to speak freely or not—becomes central to human autonomy and virtue. Our thinkers do not always trust the ability of "common people" (to borrow from Confucius) to say anything worth hearing, unless they had been prepared beforehand by the State or self-reflection. It would have been easy here to write "human happiness" instead of autonomy or virtue, but the works here are not very interested in that subject. To them happiness was an empty vessel, the credit balance from other, richer themes—freedom of choice or conscience, respect for the structure of the State and stability under it, the cultivation of belief and virtue, the balance of our personal and communal life and thought, private study and meditation. Ultimately happiness must be individually experienced, and is beyond the promises of managed public communication. Even Marx and Engels appear to take this view, when they imagine a post-revolutionary world where politics is unnecessary and true relations between people can blossom without mediation (that part of their agenda, at least, might have attracted Hayek the libertarian had he believed that their methods would accomplish this, instead of the Statist society that troubled him).

What is the relationship between PR and truth? If PR was no more than a mechanical function, this question would not be important, but these works recognized that PR activities have a life of their own, that cannot be so easily directed by a guiding hand, like a hammer or artist's brush. Al-Farabi, Gandhi and Luther believed absolute truth could be attainable, at least for some, and only after a great inner awakening, and that managed public communication could get you closer to or further from it. Confucius and Plato conceived of truth as a virtuous state guided by virtuous middle-aged (or in their time, late middle-aged) individuals with virtuous inhabitants who had been prepared by managed media to value their polity. In *The Communist Manifesto* the truth is a goal the authors are unable to describe, but which must be reached by activating a vast group by creative and disciplined propaganda. Clausewitz's truth is the reality of military rivalry, the inevitability of war and the need to prepare nation states to fight them to the end. The truths of Mill, Hayek and Jung are somewhat more nuanced, lying in a belief that human imperfection must often be tolerated, that individual autonomy— whether of personality, liberty in economic and private affairs, or psychological wellbeing—must be preserved in the face of intense and vociferous publicity techniques exercised by the State, or by people claiming to speak for immense audiences that do not really exist or obstruct individual development. These works, while in no doubt about the power of PR techniques, cannot agree on the nature of truth, only that their versions of it are currently being withheld and the management of media must therefore change.

For change to happen audiences must be created or at least identified, shown which media to use and told how to use it properly. Naturally, the works' perceptions of audiences often differ greatly from our own, because their solutions and problems reflected their own historical experience. Plato wanted to reach the *polis*, for only citizens themselves could assent to a division of new and clearly defined audiences and rulers along the lines proposed in *The Republic*. These divisions involved certain responsibilities over media management. Confucius placed that responsibility in the hands of rulers and the gentlemen who served them centrally, or in outlying regions. It was the responsibility of the rest to listen, learn and absorb, and those who did, and demonstrated some talent, could rise through the ranks. Al-Farabi placed everything in the hands of one person, or at best a small group of people who were nearly but not quite as good as the One. His audiences were the Perfected and the Imperfect. Marx and Engels, with their great audiences of bourgeois and proletariat were in some ways a throwback to this view of the world, which they persisted with despite struggling with economics-based gradations between subgroups, and with people wanting to see themselves in other ways altogether, even in Communist States. This refreshing contrariness is perhaps PR's biggest ally, and keeps it alert to new ideas and new media instead of degenerating into stale repetition of techniques and messages. Luther also created two clear sides, of the righteous individual and the corrupt Church, providing evidence for their reality. For Clausewitz the audiences were also very simple—a motivating government and motivated national citizens; having seen what the French revolutionaries and Napoleon could do, he was evidently convinced of the communication power of nation-states, and its reach. In this sense, subtlety escaped him as it did Marx and Engels. Mill, Gandhi, Hayek and Jung took a more sophisticated approach once again, in keeping with increased awareness about the role PR techniques were playing in public life. Gandhi showed how individuals could collectively direct those techniques against the State, and the other three worried about the way the State, or its supporters, directed them at the individual. All these works, concerned with public life, were not just written for a particular audience, but were manuals for showing how those in power should manage their own communication between multiple audiences.

These "manuals" contained instructions about which media should be used, and how. Invariably, they advocated media their target audiences preferred. Confucius and Plato focused on songs, ceremonies, myths, language, music and prayers, in accordance with the ritual origins of such media. Plato took a step forward—if it was forward—by advocating the need for a "noble lie" to communicate. We may imagine the reaction of Confucius to that. Al-Farabi imagined the uncritical absorption of wisdom via word-of-mouth, since perfection needs no artifice. Luther made powerful attacks on the fallen condition of religious media and demonstrated the possibilities of the printed polemic against the tattered relic. Clausewitz in *On War* anticipates a campaign to stir up individual willpower that proved as comprehensive as modern warfare itself. Marx and Engels envisaged a similar process, a combination of Luther and Clausewitz, directed on behalf of the workers of the world. Mill concentrated solely on the popular press, whose mass circulation seemed to blot out all other media platforms. Gandhi explained how a combination of techniques could be used involving publishing substantive research, vivid events, letters, pamphlets, interviews and media relations in general that was believed to embody a sincere, intelligent, collective effort. Hayek and Jung noted the intensification of PR techniques and some of the ways they could be used. Their recommendations were to restore the individual role in that process, and a consciousness that could baffle PR's alienating, un-human, dehumanizing, unhealthy tendencies.

Is this not what is happening now? Has the information age passed the instruments of mass persuasion to the individual? Can individuals now advocate products, services and ideas with as much power as organizations? Do the works featured here offer any guide to the future? Is there enough insight in them to take us that far?

Jung, Hayek and Gandhi are surest of all that there is something in us that continues to assert its psychological, economic and spiritual uniqueness, and this prevents complete assent to all collective tendencies. We are sometimes "the cat who walks alone" (to paraphrase Kipling's story) as much as we wish not to be left out. In the Information Age, this is surely an essential quality. If "truth" or "authenticity" mean anything at all, they must surely involve something individuals should experience within themselves, over and above the insistences of strategic communication. Amid the noise of the public arena, the hype of new technology, tracking devices and focus groups designed to make a mass message feel personal, the communication engines are so far unable to drill all the way into the "still small voice" of our own selves. Jung might perhaps describe that place as a combination of our spiritual centre and unique life experience, Gandhi as our instinct to make our own relationship with the Divine Will, Hayek as our will for liberty. We might recall that this voice was heard in Kings 1, 19 after the fire, the wind and earthquake: a fitting analogy for what remains after the sound and fury of PR has passed. Wherever the communicators themselves stand on the issue, the task of the individual is to avoid the fate of Parsons in Orwell's *Nineteen Eighty-Four*, uncritical believer in the communication aimed at him, finally betrayed by his own son when even he let slip a moment of scepticism. We must take care to apply this principle of individuality to products, services or causes we are inclined to endorse, as well as those we oppose. PR that is capable of working with such a principle would however be very powerful indeed, and it might also be more truthful, authentic and liberating.

Is the principle of individuality being applied today in PR, or propaganda, or strategic communication, or whatever we might call this invisible function now or in future? PR is a very strong force. The authors of the works in this book assayed the strength of its constituent elements. We have also seen that most felt the majority of people were incapable of doing anything productive with it, anything that led to a permanent, good way of living. Even Mill distrusted the collective expression of mass power coming to fruition in his time, though he understood the need for individuality to be preserved and that mass publicity could be a force for good. Marx and Engels did not suspect it, so long as it was properly used. Clausewitz recommended that the national government take control of the new passions unloosed by the rise of people Confucius, Plato and al-Farabi would have kept passive and firmly in place, if only for their own good. In *Analects* we have already seen it recorded: "The Master said, 'If excellent people managed the State for a hundred years, then certainly they could overcome cruelty and do away with executions'—how true this saying is!" (Slingerland, 2003, 13.11).

If individuals learn to use the tools organizational PR uses, as technology is already enabling them to do, the result could certainly be unwelcome. There may be yet fewer places where a "still small voice" can make itself heard. Winston Smith in *Nineteen Eighty-Four* is forced to squeeze himself into a tiny nook in his tiny apartment to escape the always-on camera, the always-on radio, the workplace propaganda sessions. Will we find ourselves in the same corner, driven there not only by large organizations, but also other individuals loudly grinding their axes? It is not only important to retain control over our personal data but also to be able to go wholly unnoticed, to be left alone from time to time, to "walk alone", in the belief that this liberty is a large part of what we are. Two verses of a Great War poem by Wilfred Owen come to mind:

> I am the ghost of Shadwell Stair.
>   Along the wharves by the water-house,
>   And through the cavernous slaughter-house,
> I am the shadow that walks there.
>
> Yet I have flesh both firm and cool,
>   And eyes tumultuous as the gems
>   Of moons and lamps in the full Thames
> When dusk sails wavering down the Pool.

(Stallworthy, 1990)

Those thinkers who tackled the communication media of the early industrial era were in no doubt that the individual must prepare for it, that the light of publicity could be useful, and that it offered alternatives to the traditional sources of authority in public communication. Those alternatives have proliferated: non-profit organizations and businesses, celebrities, local communities are making themselves heard alongside the traditional sources of states and organized religions. People can publicize things they enjoy, or oppose, from ice cream to theocracies. The next stage in this process would seem to be more intervention by individuals themselves, the "common person" who it is to be hoped lives up to Mills' hopes, rather than Plato's fears.

The next stage: but humanity is not there yet. While we as individuals are able to develop our own voice, we are still unable to guard its smallness and stillness. Not for ourselves, or our descendants. Areas of our lives that would once have passed unnoticed are now in PR's searchlight: our private conscience, our relationships, the tightening noose around product reputation and personal self-worth. The organizations, as they compete, dig deeper into us to make profound connections via target audiences large or small, via issues, corporate social responsibility, reputation management and all PR's other specialist activities. True, we too can do the same to others, thanks to social media, which will take more vivid, attractive and personal forms in future. Can we trust ourselves to do it responsibly? It is big organizations, however, which continue to have resources and time to coordinate large, long-term and consistent campaigns—another facet of PR's reality, or dream, that flows unaltered from past to present.

References

Arendt, H. (1973) *The Origins of Totalitarianism*. New York: Harcourt Brace Jovanovich.

Bernays, E. L. (2005) *Propaganda*. New York: Ig Publishing.

Camus, A. (1956) *The Rebel: An Essay on Man in Revolt*. New York: Vintage Books.

Demetrious, K. (2013) *Public Relations, Activism, and Social Change: Speaking Up*. New York: Routledge.

Harding, L. (2009) "Russia Today Launches First UK Ad Blitz." *The Guardian*, December 18. Retrieved from www.theguardian.com/world/2009/dec/18/russia-today-propaganda-ad-blitz.

Moloney, K. (2006) *Rethinking Public Relations: PR Propaganda and Democracy*. London: Routledge.

Moore, S. (1996) *An Invitation to Public Relations*. London: Cassell.

More, T. (1992) *Utopia*. New York: Knopf.

Stallworthy, J. (1990) *Wilfred Owen: The War Poems*. London: Chatto & Windus.

Slingerland, E. (2003) *Confucius Analects*. Indianapolis, IN: Hackett Publishing Company.

Index

Taylor & Francis

eBooks

FOR LIBRARIES

ORDER YOUR FREE 30 DAY INSTITUTIONAL TRIAL TODAY!

Over 23,000 eBook titles in the Humanities, Social Sciences, STM and Law from some of the world's leading imprints.

Choose from a range of subject packages or create your own!

Benefits for you

▶ Free MARC records
▶ COUNTER-compliant usage statistics
▶ Flexible purchase and pricing options

Benefits for your user

▶ Off-site, anytime access via Athens or referring URL
▶ Print or copy pages or chapters
▶ Full content search
▶ Bookmark, highlight and annotate text
▶ Access to thousands of pages of quality research at the click of a button

For more information, pricing enquiries or to order a free trial, contact your local online sales team.

UK and Rest of World: **online.sales@tandf.co.uk**

US, Canada and Latin America:
e-reference@taylorandfrancis.com

www.ebooksubscriptions.com

ALPSP Award for BEST eBOOK PUBLISHER 2009 Finalist

Taylor & Francis eBooks
Taylor & Francis Group

A flexible and dynamic resource for teaching, learning and research.

For Product Safety Concerns and Information please contact our EU
representative GPSR@taylorandfrancis.com
Taylor & Francis Verlag GmbH, Kaufingerstraße 24, 80331 München, Germany

www.ingramcontent.com/pod-product-compliance
Ingram Content Group UK Ltd.
Pitfield, Milton Keynes, MK11 3LW, UK
UKHW021609240425
457818UK00018B/469